GET UP
GIRL!

Made for Success Publishing
P.O. Box 1775 Issaquah, WA 98027
www.MadeForSuccess.com

Distributed by Made for Success Publishing

First Printing
Library of Congress Cataloging-in-Publication data
McFarland, Sarah
Get Up Girl!: Release Your Roar!
p. cm.

LCCN: 2023943992
ISBN: 978-1-64146-797-1 *(PBBK)*
ISBN: 978-1-64146-798-8 *(eBook)*

Printed in the United States of America

For further information contact Made for Success Publishing
+1425-526-6480 or email service@madeforsuccess.net

GET UP
GIRL!

RELEASE YOUR ROAR!

Have the courage to pursue your dreams
and overcome those obstacles in *business* and
life. Everything on the other side of you is
waiting for you to get back up!

SARAH MCFARLAND

Get UP!

Fight!

Get Beat

Rise

Repeat

Get UP!

Fight!

Get Beat

Rise...

Overcome

WIN!

This book is dedicated to my daughter, Victoria. May you grow in wisdom, strength, and humility. May your journeys take you to new places, and may the doors of favor be ever open to you. I pray you will always feel loved, free, upright, courageous, and kind. Whenever you fall, be quick to get back up, and always be the fearless dreamer and the persistent victor. Victoria, may you never lose your "Roar!"

CONTENTS

Chapter 1

FINDING YOUR
ROAR AGAIN!

L IFE ISN'T ABOUT HOW MANY TIMES YOU FALL. IT IS ABOUT HOW many times you get back up! And you *will* get back up. And when you do get back up, you will be the bigger, badder, and stronger 2.0 version of who you are called to be! I wrote this book to share with you my journey on what worked at times and what also worked against me. By the end of reading this book, you will value yourself more, have improved boundaries, know your identity better and be more courageous, wiser, focused, and determined than ever before! You will find purpose and re-ignite your dream again! Together, we will go back to the drawing board. You will get a vision, and I will give you the tools required so that you can be healthy and strong enough to execute the goals needed to fulfill that dream! We are going back to find purpose, back to find healing, and back to find your voice! It's time to release your "Roar!"

This book is for the dreamer that finds themselves stuck somewhere between apathy and lost hope. This book is for the female entrepreneur with doors that seem like they are always out of reach. This book is for the world changer that settles for lost purpose and unscaled mountains, settling in valleys too low to climb out of. This book is for the woman, running on empty, desperately trying to get to the finish line. This book is for the thirsty ones, the *ones* who don't know how, but are willing to fight in the name of passion and purpose. You will be the ones that will *pioneer*! You will be the *trailblazers* that chart new paths, and you will learn to break through the barriers and rise above every self-inflicted limitation. This book is for the *overcomers*. I have overcome, and so will you. This book was written for you!

My background isn't in writing or psychology, and I am not the most successful businessperson out there. I am, however, a female entrepreneur who lost what I would call was my "*Roar*," and I got stuck as so many women often do at times. I lost my passion. I settled for defeat and couldn't seem to find my confidence again. I was where we find ourselves on the road, in the pursuit of success. I was metaphorically driving with a broken-down car and no place to go.

This book won't offer a ten-step guide to finding success in business or a three-step process to finding inner peace… Sometimes, life isn't all that easy, and if it were, you wouldn't be reading this book! I have often found that we will look for the answers all around us, even though we know that they can't be found in the places we are looking at or through the people we are asking.

The answers are far too complicated for your business partners, your friends, your mentors, or even your pastors to unravel. And so, we lose hope. We just settle, and we keep searching for what we do not understand. We search for things that are circumstantial when the answers are not around us but are most often within us.

This book is about the journey we go through in business, and the obstacles we face, while going through life to find the best version of who we can be! It's just life, and there isn't always a masterclass to take on how to thrive in it. Business is complex, and being a female entrepreneur isn't easy. There are many daily challenges we have to hurdle and obstacles we must surpass.

I wrote this book to inspire you to *get back up* and find out who you are meant to be on the other side of getting up. It was written to spark a fire and help you find your purpose and calling! This book will challenge you. It should make you feel uncomfortable and encourage you to find healing in places that you may not want to. This book will get you to face your demons and take down those giants standing in front of you so that you can be the great entrepreneur you are called to be in a challenging era that you are meant to overcome! The desire to write this book is not just to help women see who they can become but also to help raise up a generation of fearless leaders that are different than the generations that came before us. We are living in a challenging era. Accordingly, we will need to be able to pivot from the past, to go forward into the future.

These are extremely complicated and pressing times that we are living in, and the ability to change and adapt is crucial. I believe that young people are looking for hope and something to believe in. I also believe that *you* have the capability to be that hope dealer! My generation (the Millennials) and the younger generations (Generation Z and Alpha) have the aptitude to do great things.

But in order to do so, we will have to adapt, face some fears and chart new paths, but I also believe our generations will be the next "Greatest Generations" of women! I believe that we will be the generations that "overcome!" We are living in a remarkable moment, and it is an incredible time for women coming up in the world. Women in the Alpha- Millennial generations may very well produce some of the most significant business leaders of all time in the marketplace, and in it, we are stronger together.

Who am I? I am a wife and a mother, a sister, a daughter, a fellow cheerleader, an entrepreneur, a humanitarian, and a lifelong student. As women, we are many things, and we wear many hats. In my capacity as a female entrepreneur, I am a land developer and an investor. I have created and owned businesses since I was 26 years old. I also made my first million dollars when I was 32. Before that, I was either in school or worked for other people. The road hasn't always been easy, nor has it always been friendly. I had no road map, easy way up, or money. I faced a lot of trials and a whole lot of rejection. I have been through every imaginable obstacle and, perhaps, like many of you, have suffered them in silence. But I did make it through, and when beaten down, I did get back up, and I am standing strong again! I didn't allow being stuck to be the end of the road for me. I chose to pivot and find my "Roar" again.

What is your "Roar"? A "Roar" is where your confidence and strength come from. It is said that the roar of a lion can be heard up to 5 miles away! Lions and Lionesses communicate by roaring to measure their opposition after listening to how many roars they can hear back. It is a territorial marking relating to occupying an area.

The "Roar" is your courage! It represents your battle cry, the ability to stand amidst fear, fight for victories, and take new ground! It showcases your power and might. The singer and Feminist Icon, Helen Reddy, coined the term and sang the song in 1972, "I Am Woman, Hear Me Roar." Helen Reddy created an anthem and began a movement for women voicing the injustices towards them. This song was the battle cry for the Women's Liberation Movement of the 1960's to the 1980's. Gloria Steinem championed it early on, which helped to mobilize women fighting for equality in western nations. As a result, women have achieved a greater level of social equality. This movement also changed how women were perceived and represented regarding political and socio-economic status.

Listen to that song and let it be your battle cry. Helen Reddy understood social inequality's injustices and did her part to change the world through just one song. Her contributions still impact us today. She sang that she had been broken. She sang that she had to learn from her pain and found strength in pursuing her goals through it. Settling for less when you know there is more… is not an option. You may have to be willing to stand firm during difficult periods of time, but if you do, who knows how your contributions may change the world we live in.

When you lose your "Roar," it means that you know what it's like to have had it, and that means that you can go back and find it. When you look for it, you will most likely find it right where you dropped it. And when you do get it back, your "Roar" will be heard louder and go further than ever before!

So, go get that "Roar" again! Allow me to share with you how I rose above my struggles, got out of my valleys, and climbed those mountains. Let me be your cheerleader! We can walk through this daily and make it as intimate as you want. Set a time to meet with me in a comfortable place in your home, and *let's begin the dialogue*. We will start together and find healing daily. We will get through this transformative time with each other because *you* are not alone. We will stand strong again and get up once more!

Invite me to come with you as we journey to find victory. Not only will you scale that mountain, but you *will* plant your flag at the top! I have been where you are and want to go with you to find real value, and I want to challenge you to get back up again. Let us build up healthy women, not only within ourselves but also for those around us. We need to raise up healed generations that will lead with strength, courage, honor, and kindness, and you are part of that call! Your destinations are limitless! Let's kill those giants, close those deals, run those boardrooms, and win together! I invite you to join me on this journey as we raise up the next generation of fearless dreamers and level up to new heights! Let's find your "ROAR!"

Chapter 2

GO TO NINEVEH

IT'S BEEN THREE YEARS SINCE I LAST CONTRIBUTED TO WRITING this book. I started out wanting to write and inspire young women and entrepreneurs in business. I wanted to share with them how to overcome obstacles by sharing how I had. And honestly, it looked a lot different than it does now. I had to start back at Chapter One and re-write the whole thing. So here I am... amending what I wrote several years ago. In order to go forward, sometimes we have to go backward, and when we can't find what we are looking for, often, it will be right where we dropped it.

When you are called to do something, do it! Don't run away from it. The consequences of resisting your calling are always greater. You just have to go for it, no matter how much you don't want to. In the bible, there is a story about a man named Jonah. He was told by God to go to Nineveh. He didn't want to go. In the process of rejecting God's plan, he ended up getting swallowed by a whale. He also ended up going to Nineveh, taken by the very whale that swallowed him up... Think about that. In the story,

God literally sent a whale to go and get Jonah and bring him back to where he was supposed to be. The moral of the story... Go to your Nineveh, and you will avoid the whale and get to where you are going much faster!

Why am I sharing Jonah's story at the beginning of mine? Because I was like a *Jonah* and this book was my *Nineveh*. And although I didn't start out like a Jonah, I found myself becoming one in the process. So here I am today, finishing what I was supposed to anyways. But it certainly wasn't easy, and it cost me just about everything to come back to you. I found myself unraveling through the writing of this book. It was as though the Universe was saying, "Well, you're going to write it, but you will write it my way! Everything you have learned isn't all wrong but needs to be revised." The re-writing of this book took me several years. It was indubitably a transfiguration and a reprogramming of who would be needed to carry the weight of what I was trying to bring to the finish line.

When I first started, I was writing a book on overcoming and teaching others to get back up. Until that point, I had faced a great degree of obstacles and wanted to write a book on how to face those difficult times. However, by writing this book, I was setting into motion my very own journey. In doing so, a new set of challenges emerged that I would have to go through for my *own* self to *get back up*. Writing this book helped me find my identity. In a significant way, it was therapy. There was a more profound journey that I needed to go through in order to almost *earn* the privilege of writing such a book, and that journey was not complete.

Unlike Jonah, I did start by going in the right direction, but after some difficulty, I found myself, like him, running away. So even when we try and start off on the right foot, whether you like it or not, you better bring a raincoat, an umbrella, or perhaps the whole damn storm shelter. Because, like it or not, there will be storms! You will get off course at times, and you may even jump ship in the process.

This is what happened to me. I was slightly younger and full of pride, and I did not carry my successes well. I was at the top of my game in 2019, pre-Covid. I was working on a land development project with a parcel of land I had purchased the previous year. That year was one of the best earning years I had up until that point, and I already made my first million before I was 32 years old. For someone who had to grind for it and didn't come from money, that was a lot for me. This was also pre-Covid inflation.

In addition, before that, I had seen nothing but a level of success in all my entrepreneurial endeavors. It wasn't easy, but there was a reasonably positive track record from early on. So, I decided to write a book and share my story. I also decided to start a foundation for women called "Let Love Be Greater." This foundation was created to give women and children who are at an economic and socioeconomic disadvantage scholarship opportunities and financial aid. Because I thought that's what you do when you reach some level of success. You write a book to share your journey and start a foundation with a dream to change the world! Well, the devil was in the details… and I got stuck on Chapter 5. After that, the unraveling became me. My life came to a screeching halt. It was as though the devil himself had asked me,

"How dare you write a book teaching women how to get up?" and poured me a strong glass of what I was writing.

If you let it, the world will keep you down, and I absolutely 100% did! I threw my own pity party, took out a bag of popcorn, and watched the unfolding movie of a train wreck… and I was the main star. Then, after the best earnings year came the worst, and I thought to myself, "The audacity of writing this book!" As aforementioned, I got stuck on Chapter 5. The very thing I was writing about seemed to have become the very thing I needed to be rescued from.

Doors seemed to just start shutting simultaneously. Covid slowed land development sales significantly. After I formed the non-profit in 2020, I then just stared at it for the next season of my life and cried like the victim I let myself become. It was pathetic. I was overwhelmed and could not take on one more thing. I was so overwhelmed because I wouldn't allow myself any help. I wouldn't allow any help because I was so full of pride. I was full of pride because it was a mask for fear. I lived in fear because I held on to unhealed mindsets and false teachings. Unhealed mindsets, coupled with false teachings, are dangerous things to harbor. It is the lens through which we view life and operate from. This lens then creates the truths and belief systems that we navigate from.

There is this stigma about women. We feel that to be successful, we must do things on our own… shatter the glass ceilings on our own. Be strong and independent on our own. Conquer the world… *on our own*. The dilemma here is that we create an enemy that does not need to exist and operate from a victim mindset that is false and limiting. This modern-day feminism would not exist without an antagonist. Who is the antagonist? That antagonist becomes everyone you perceive as a threat, including men and even those who genuinely want to help you. The problem wasn't that I didn't know these truths. I genuinely was raised to be independent in a very "pretty way." And when I say pretty, pretty like a lady. Like I could still be traditional and yet be independent and strong, still be classy but have that seat at the table. Go into the boardroom, but wear those stilettos too. So, I hated modern-day feminism. I saw it as the true antagonist for women and the family unit. You could say that I was even rebellious to these principles and set out to prove that you could be a feminine lady and still operate in business and thrive.

It's not that modern-day feminism never found a place to flourish in society because it certainly did. Forms of it were also more relatable to a specific audience during specified time periods. I just feel like at this moment in my life, it isn't entirely relatable to me, or perhaps my generation, and is in need of a major facelift. I think it's time we evolve as women! Somewhere along the line, modern-day feminism pivoted towards something much darker and angrier than I was willing to embrace. I saw the principles behind it as esoteric and destructive against what I wanted to build in my own life. It was more of a movement that served the 90's, and like the 90's… went out with the 90's and is never coming back in style.

My Father taught me to expect the door to be opened and the seat to be pulled out. It's not old-fashioned. It's just class and knowing your value and your worth. Yes, I am very capable of opening my *own* door, and I can run to do it, to prove it too. But I expect to exude a certain level of etiquette, and there is nothing weak about living with those expectations. Nor am I any less an independent and strong woman because of it. That way of thinking is contributing to so much dysfunction and role obfuscation in America today.

Let me preface with, "I grew up as the quintessential tomboy." And while working, I have been knee-deep in mud and sewers, working with contractors. I have negotiated with the best of them. I have also had to fight and handle three separate legal cases almost simultaneously in one season of my life. I could go on and on. In no way or form was I a *fragile flower*. At the same time, I have also chosen to make dinners for my husband regularly, chosen to let him lead our house in many of our affairs, and chosen to let him be the man of our home. There is nothing weak about building up your man and allowing him to feel… like a man, like a partner and a friend. Neither am I less of an empowering woman by doing so.

And yes, as an independent woman, I could pay on dates, lead with angry eyebrows, and join the movement to emasculate our men, but I don't want to. There is something special about allowing a man to just be a man, and a woman, a woman, and keeping some forms of traditional and classical values while updating other more obsolete and esoteric ones. There is a time and a place to be a lady and be elegant, and there is a time and a place to be "boss" and be that *warrior*. Choosing both does not equate to you being weak either! When we lose identity in the roles we play, we lose the value of who we are, and then roles can become very confusing and burdensome.

Because of my father, I was taught that there are no limitations and that the only limitations are the ones you place upon yourself. I am a daughter of an Army Ranger who graduated from the military academy, The Citadel. My father epitomizes character and strength and has a certain mental fortitude that is quite rare. I was taught to be strong. However, there were times that even though I was raised a certain way, I found myself reverting to false teachings and false narratives that we, as women, are constantly inundated with. When you find yourself in moments of weakness, all the junk comes out. If you allow it, even the sheer strength of your foundation can crack. And you might find yourself settling for a Snickers bar when you have a chocolate soufflé at home. What's your *Snickers bar*? What have you settled for and lost out on?

We are constantly bombarded with a victim mindset in our culture. It helps to breed the division that we currently live in. It also gives us an excuse to stay stuck and down. So, we have to re-train the way we think. Everything we are learning teaches us that complacency is ok and that our failure is someone else's fault. So, this movement that means to unite and strengthen us really just divides and teaches us to operate from the point of weakness.

Victimhood results in a mindset where you don't succeed because you think nothing will work, and nothing will change. You are looking for an excuse to stop working towards success, and instead of looking for ways around problems, you look for excuses to find problems and stop working as a result. This is soul-crushing! You will eventually end up with no desire to succeed or advance, and if you do it long enough, you will have no ability to succeed or advance. It becomes a self-fulfilling prophecy and a way of life. It becomes an engrained mental state. Failure becomes your state of mind when success should be your state of mind.

Modern-day feminism tells you that to be strong; you must accept that you are weak and a victim. Later, you can then pride yourself on overcoming those limitations that restrict you. There has to be someone pushing you down for you to be able to come up. It's a lonely concept and quite isolating. But if no antagonists existed, some of these organizations would have no purpose, so they created the *war*. Having worked in politics when I was younger, I learned how some of these NPOs and "Think Tanks" operate, build their market, and make their money. They have to solve a problem, and if one doesn't exist, they will create one.

Modern-day feminism is anything but empowering and has become both radicalized and monetized. Why can't we believe in empowering women, just to empower and cheerlead each other? Why can't we let men fit into our equation in a healthy space?

So, why did I allow these victim mindsets to creep in? Well, at this moment in my life, I was out to prove to the world that I would do it on my own, and so I did. I did do it on my own, and I struggled on my own at times too. And when the unraveling began, it was no one else's unraveling but mine and it was a lonely place to be. This type of thinking is toxic and can be characteristic of a *fortress mentality*. Fortress mentality or siege mentality occurs when people feel as though they are under attack and tend to protect themselves from any criticisms or viewpoints that do not align with their own. It is a shared mentality of defensiveness and victimization. There is no space in the workplace for this type of thinking. When you work on your own, you will break on your own… and on your own, you can only go so far until you exhaust yourself!

At this point, I was two years into a new marriage, four years out from an old one, recovering from a difficult divorce and legal battle to sell the shares of a company I owned, and coming in HOT from a season of raising two children on my own. Since the age of 18, I have been running a race, not like a marathon, but like a very fast sprint. It started with going to college, where I worked several jobs, interned at a local news station, and wrote for my school newspaper. Then it was "off to work," working in politics, drafting bill legislation, and doing research. Then, it was "Chief of Staff" for a state-elected official. After that, it was marriage, kids, a master's degree, and starting two companies back-to-back. Some of these were simultaneous events. I was running so fast that I ran through the most challenging season of my life, my divorce. During this season, I just continued to do what I always did, which was to sprint. I ran unhealed, and so these mindsets crept in and began to take over my thinking. I had to do it all on my own. You have to understand; I was coming from a season where I had to fight for things being taken from me… literally.

I was the VP of a company one day and received a letter through certified mail the next, stating that I would be stripped of my title and distributions all in one moment. This was from a company that I owned. I was being pushed and pressured to be bought out. I thought I had every right to be the victim I allowed myself to be. But business is just business sometimes, and it's not for everyone! There is always a bottom line and companies have to run at a profit. However, as a single mother of two children, there is no limit to what you will do to provide for your kids. When things get tough, you have to get tougher. So, I went into fight mode, and I ended up getting what I wanted in the end, but it came at a cost.

I didn't stop to rest there, either. Shortly after, I ran into a new marriage, not even having the time to recover from a divorce. I picked up a new venture and began the whole cycle again. I began a land development project as the lead developer and started selling individual lots. Then, Covid happened. It put a halt to everything. I could no longer run fast, and it became eerily quiet.

What happened during Covid was that I had to face who I was in the quiet… without everything that I had built myself up to be. The effects of Covid stripped down the ego, the identity in business, and the false sense of security. It made me deal with who I was at my very core.

When your foundation is shaken, you will find what you are truly made out of. I hated who I was, and who I was, at my core, was a runner. Up to this point, the same brokenness and inadequacies existed, but the runner in me was always able to outrun the stillness. I was in survival mode, which carried me so far, but the runner was always there. Even in my past successes, I was just able to cover it up a little easier because I was running so fast. Quickly moving from one success to the next, never staying long enough to commit beyond the building of it. Long enough to create something great but not long enough to build something that lasts. Staying in something too long meant that I would have to believe in myself, which was more than what I had to offer at that time. The victim mindset was just a symptom of a more systemic issue. I didn't like who I was because I didn't believe in myself. I didn't believe in myself because I didn't know who I was. I had an *identity* problem.

By no means am I saying that what I had achieved until that point was a failure. It just wasn't as great as it could have been. So, I stopped writing. Even though I felt called to write this book. I didn't want to anymore. How could I write a book teaching women how to be fearless entrepreneurs when I felt like I had not lived up to my own measures of success?

Within the same year, the development did sell, but I had already stopped writing by then. I believe, at that time, it even sold for one of the highest prices per square foot in the area for horizontal land development. By all standards of worldly measurement, the project was a success. But was it as successful as I had wanted it to be? No, and that was the problem. I was a perfectionist and measured my worth and value by my personal standards. It just didn't measure up, and when your only self-worth is in what you do, what happens when what you do isn't enough?

My original plan was to build houses on the 16 lots that were platted out in my project. Prior to this, I had just spent the past year and a half working on engineering, rezoning, platting, grading, designing, and negotiating. A lot of hard work went into it. Covid temporarily paused the sales, and I didn't have an adequate financing plan to account for that. But really, who could have accounted for Covid? I was left with the decision to either find a new financing partner or sell the development in its entirety, and I went with the latter out of fear. I sold that project, and it took a dream away from me. I sold myself short, and it was not an easy sale, but I didn't believe in myself enough then to hold on to it. So, I did what we often do in the face of fear, and I settled. The difficulty of the development, the disappointments, and the past decade just seemed to pile in on me all at once. I couldn't go another inch. The past 15 years of just doing and running the race left me unfueled and running on empty. I had nothing left to give, I had been pouring out my whole career, and when the quiet came, the storm set in. I sold the development and knew I just needed to rest and reset.

For the next year and a half, I felt paralyzed and was aware that deeper work would need to be done if I was going to move forward. I took a break from working and began to face who I really was. I knew that without facing who I was, I would just keep running because I was running from myself. The truth was, I didn't believe in me. Was it validated? No, I had a decent resume at that point, but the problem was that I had an *identity crisis* and didn't honestly know who I was. So, as long as I didn't know who I was, there was room for every past lie and label to come in and tell me that I was not enough.

If you don't know who you are, you will leave room for the world to tell you who you are. I believe it is our generation's greatest crisis. We don't know who we are. Therefore, we don't know what we are capable of. I felt inadequate. I was like a lion without my "Roar!" I couldn't seem to find my courage again. Who I said I was mattered. What I thought about myself impacted my perceived reality. I lacked faith in who I was. I was a businesswoman, and aside from that, I didn't know anything else. It all seemed to hit me at once, and it was as if my soul was asking me to take a moment for myself just to heal. So that is what I did. After the sale of the development, I stopped doing. I stopped looking for a new project. I stopped writing and just took a pause.

I needed that pause… But this story is so much more than what I went through, and this book isn't about how I became the most successful entrepreneur out there because I am clearly not! There are far too many more qualified that run substantial companies with thousands of employees. There are also a million books selling you on success and how to reach it, and this is not that type of book. This is just me sharing the pitfalls of a journey where my accomplishments would only carry me so far and, in that journey, how I found my courage again. How I learned to look inside and to like that person I saw in the mirror.

Because what happens when you fall before you reach where you are trying to go? What happens when you reach a measure of success and fall in the pursuit of your master plan? What happens if you fall, can't find the "how" or the "why," and lose the passion and the purpose? What happens when too many closed doors break your spirit, and you can't find the courage to open one more door? So, you just stop dreaming. Because it's better to get by than to have crushed dreams… Rejection is a painful thing, and hope deferred will make any heart sick.

This is a story about how I got up, and finishing my book is a part of my journey in getting up. This is your story about how you get up, how we get up together. And you will get up! The unraveling can be a good thing. Sometimes the best gifts come through the worst moments of chaos, and it is there, that we find the good stuff! Not just the bad. Leave the bad but keep the good! Face the storms. The storms shake us. They test us. They temper us. Like steel in a forge, we become harder and more resilient. There is good in the storms. They help us to understand who we are in them. I believe storms can give us an opportunity to pivot and to re-direct our course. They give us the ability to see the things that we do not like and make the changes that are needed to be made. Don't get swallowed up by the storms, and accept the delay. Ride the storms out. Most likely, you will end up where you need to get to, but what will you lose in the delay? Don't accept delay!

When Jonah got to Nineveh, the story in the bible said that he helped to save a nation of people! So, who is on the other side of your storm? What humanitarian assignment, business venture, or dream are you delaying that can change someone's life and impact the world if you just *get up*? Overcome what tied you up in the first place and get to where you are supposed to go. Don't run around that mountain over and over again while you watch your peers circle the top. Summit the mountain! You weren't created to watch them. You were created to run with them. This is the moment you overcome! This is the moment you *get up*! Believe in yourself. I believe in you! I believe in everything on the other side of you getting up. Dream with me again. Re-ignite your purpose because the best is yet to come!

Chapter 3

HAVE COURAGE
AND BE KIND

I AM A PRODUCT OF THE "DISNEY GENERATION." I ABSOLUTELY loved Cinderella, Sleeping Beauty, and everything Disney! My favorite quote even comes from the modern-day Cinderella with Lily James, "Have Courage and Be Kind." This is such a powerful statement and story. As we all know, Cinderella was picked on and ridiculed by everyone around her, including her own family. Just to preface… I love my family, and they do not pick on me! So, how did she handle it? With courage and with kindness. She chose the higher path and allowed her circumstances to play out. She did not respond to what was happening around her and did not allow the torment of her sisters and step mother to dictate who she would be. Neither did she lower her standards of elegance and grace in who she was, despite an extraordinarily deplorable and despotic situation.

Cinderella was a woman of elegance and class who knew who she was. She may have had to clean the toilet and be everyone's servant, but her station in life didn't supersede or dictate who she knew she was called to be. Our station in life does not get to define who we are! The girl who starts life in a drug-addicted or abusive home may even attend Harvard or Wharton one day. Those accomplishments may be reached in spite of those seemingly impossible circumstances!

Cinderella was certainly not a victim. She was an overcomer! So, when Cinderella had a little help from her *Fairy God Mother*, she was able to believe in herself. Imagine the director re-writing the script, with Cinderella telling the Fairy God Mother that she wasn't going to the ball, wasn't worthy of the prince, and decided to stay home after all? The story would have looked a lot different, but Cinderella did get to the ball, did dance with her Prince, fell in love, and the rest is fantasy! Nowhere in it were moments where Cinderella was vacillating with who she was. I understand that Cinderella is a fairytale, and we aren't all born to be a "Megan Markle." However, the truth is the same. What if there had been *Fairy God Mother's* in your life? Would you have believed in them? How can you receive help if you don't think you are worthy of it or can't see yourself dreaming, not of where you are, but of where you could be? The underlying issue often isn't that help is not available. It is that if it were, would we be able to recognize and receive it?

Knowing your value is essential. Knowing who you are and not who others say you are, is very powerful. In today's generation, if you don't know who you are, you leave room for the world to categorize and label you. There is an entire agenda that is capitalizing on just that. Without your identity, you will lose your voice. When you lose your voice, you lose your value. When you lose your value, you lose your passion, and when you lose your passion, you will lose your fight. When you lose your fight, that is a dangerous place to be at. It is extremely difficult to get back up when you have no *fight* in you. Who you say you are matters! Believing in you is the greatest gift that you can give yourself! Standing out from the crowd, being different, being who you were born to be, and loving that unique gift of a person that you are, is vital because life is too brutal, and if you let it, it *will* find a way to tear you down.

But a woman who knows her value, that can stand up amidst the boos of a crowd, a woman who can stand out *from the crowd*. My Goodness, what a force to be reckoned with! A woman that can fall, and get back up… fall, and then get back up… fall, and then yes, get back up again! That is a fierce woman! A woman with fight in her, who stands amid opposition and chooses to dance in the middle of her storms! A woman who finds her courage in the weakest of moments and knows her worth and her value? That is a rare treasure, and she will have "her crown."

When I was going through a difficult time in my life, I could not seem to find joy. Sometimes, the peace and beauty of life just seem to escape us. I remember trying to practice being grateful every day. It was the little things that helped me to remember. I used to remind myself that I had clean water, electricity, food to eat, healthy children, a house over my head, and a running car. That is more than what most people have in this world, and I had so much more than that. So, I started to see the *little things* again. I began to be grateful. Once I started appreciating life for what truly mattered, the storms didn't seem so bad anymore. The "little things" that we often forget to be thankful for are honestly so much *bigger* than what we account for. The big things... the job, the divorce, the bankruptcy, the lost deal, etc. really don't even compare to having running water, electricity, and your health. Think about that for a minute...

I remember being at the epicenter of this moment and having my car break down in the middle of the highway. I had a brand new BMW, and the computer just stopped working. But this wasn't all of it. This was after two minor fender benders. One car back-ended me at a stop light while my vehicle was parked. Another car, I ran into, in a school pickup line. This was all within two weeks of each other and on the heels of a challenging transition. When my car stopped, I was able to veer off to the side as it died, and I just started laughing! I started laughing and talking out loud like the *madwoman* I was at the moment, and I said, "Devil, is this all you've got!" I may very well have been at my breaking point. Whatever it was, on that day, I promised myself that I would not give my trials one more tear. I chose to be grateful and see the *actual* "big things" in life that I often took for granted. I began to shift and turn around my thinking. From that moment on, I began to dance and laugh in the middle of my storms! I wouldn't let one more day go, worrying over the things that I could not control.

You were born to be that woman, and this is that defining moment, "Have Courage and Be Kind." Have the Courage to get back up and face the giants standing before you! Have the kindness to give grace to those that hurt and disappoint you.

Even if it seems impossible, and even if they don't deserve it. That pain hurts you more than it does them, so it's time to remove that blockage. The famous Dalai Llama stated, "Be kind whenever possible. It is always possible."

If you don't know where to start, and have been searching to find where you lost your courage, your passion and your voice, start by going back. Go back to the place where you lost it because that is most likely where you will find it. Go back to the time that your dream was stolen. Go back to the place you lost your passion. Go back to the moment you lost your voice, and fight to get it back. Do everything you need to do to get your voice back because you deserve it… and you are so worth it, and when you come back, come back with a *"Roar"* that is so loud that even those that doubted you would have to pivot and want to cheer you!

The problem with not knowing who you are is that you will begin to believe the narrative of the world, and there is no room for courage in it. The narratives surrounding us are all negative, angry, victimizing, and depressing. Where is the space to have hope, courage, and dreams? Don't let the lies be greater than the truth of who you can be. And if resentment is holding you back, then forgive them. Forgiveness frees the forgiver. Hatred enslaves the hater. Don't let your past mistakes define, limit and restrict who you want to become, so forgive yourself too!

"Have Courage and Be Kind," means to be kind to yourself as well! Your past does not define you, your mistakes don't make you. Who you are, isn't who they say you are, or the past "broken you," say that you are either. What is your truth? Who do you dream that you are? Who do you say that you are? What is your value?

Your truths have power. What you believe about yourself can either catapult or limit you. If you stop answering the questions of this world and begin to ask your own, you will slowly drown out the narrative of it. When you start doing that, you will soon find that you have stopped becoming a robot and a slave to ideas that are not your own. You will then begin creating the world you want to live in.

You can't have both. You can't try to fit in and yet, at the same time, stand out. You have to choose one. And if you decide to stand out, accept that it may be difficult and lonely at times but that you will probably like this version of yourself much better than the version you were groomed to be. To have courage, you will have to block out the desire to fit in at times because you will be on the road less traveled. To have courage means that you will have to face your *giants* and overcome your fears. You will be up against the status quo and will go against the tide. Great thinkers and great leaders are made from decisive moments in time. How they stood in those moments shaped who they became. If Martin Luther King Jr., Abraham Lincoln, Rosa Parks, Mother Theresa and Gandhi never chose to stand out, the world would look like a vastly different place!

Will you have the courage to be different? Will you dare to run against the world's rhythm and follow the road less traveled? If you are always running with the world, how will you differentiate yourself from it? How will you allow that moment of greatness to be born? Inside each of us is greatness waiting to have its moment. And to gain the world but lose your soul... Don't choose the world. Choose yourself! Believe in yourself and stand up for who you are. Value who you are!

What was it that you lost? What caused you to drop your dreams and lose your courage, voice, fight, and passion? What is standing in the middle of your victory? What comes between you and your breakthrough? Was it exhaustion from getting back up so many times, or was it something deeper? If you can answer this question, I believe you are halfway there. Was it the loss of a loved one, a tragedy, a divorce, a bankruptcy, your own false belief system, or just a culmination of events in life? To move forward, you will have to know what took you backward. You will have to know what took you out. You must find your *fight* so you can get your voice back. Things that are lost and stolen need to be found and fought for. So, what was it?

In my case, there were several factors. I had been getting up and charging forward for a long time. Part of it was that I just needed a reset and some balance. The other parts were something much deeper, where fear and unhealed mindsets began to settle on me. It wasn't the development that broke me. It was everything that led up to that. I had been falling down and getting up, falling down and getting back up for so long. I dealt with doors that would constantly close and would have to find new ones to open. I would knock and knock until the right opportunities were found. I had to deal with the difficulties associated with being a minority female entrepreneur and continuously pioneer new areas. Being a woman, among only men in very masculine fields, can be a lonely place. Whatever it was, I always found myself fighting to break through. Whether it was distribution, politics, shipping and logistics, land development, etc. And the egos... the sabotage, the backstabbing, jealousy, and the pride you are inundated with, and having to navigate. It can be daunting!

I believe that wherever there is money, there is greed. Wherever there is greed, a greater level of discernment is needed to navigate successfully. The cycle had worn me down, and I never had the rest I needed. I also didn't have a strong enough identity to continue maintaining what I was walking in, and more importantly, where I wanted to go. Just desiring success isn't enough. Just checking off accomplishments won't satisfy you. Some of the loneliest people in the world are some of the wealthiest. You have to know who you are and what you are fighting for. You have to believe in yourself, have a purpose, and know your "Why?"

Something happened when the effects of Covid hit, and the quietness occurred. There was no success to hide in. My whole life was hidden in accomplishments up until that point. I was forced to stop running. When I stopped running, all the fear, doubt, and labels from past seasons just seemed to bubble up and marinate with me. I paused long enough to deal with my *own* self and found that I honestly didn't like who I was. So, I was forced to go on a journey to discover who I needed to be. From it, I chose to pivot in some areas so that when I came back, I would like who I saw and have a greater self-identity in who I had become. When you run so fast, you can cover up your inadequacies with marriage, ministry, position, titles, kids, a business, social calendars, and for some, even substances and alcohol. If you let them, they can all be masks. They were for me.

You have to learn to like yourself. You are born into this world alone, and you will die alone. Liking yourself is crucial, and I did not. Having faith in who you are, is what gives you courage. I didn't have faith in who I was, so I lost my courage. Because I didn't know my identity, I let what others thought about me, and just the general difficulty of life bring me down.

Before I sold the entire development, I came into financing challenges. I had finished most of the project with sewer, grading, and paving already done. I also had sold a parcel of land before paving was even finished, which was a rarity where I was developing. At that time, the sale of just the "one lot" was one of the highest per square foot in the area. It was marketed as a modern luxury development, and it was on the cutting edge of design. The partners I had in engineering and design were the best in that state. I was off to a great start, and then Covid hit. The sales got quiet, and the bank got loud. I needed to output more money or restructure my loan to keep the development going. When the lot sold, it was November of 2019, almost nine months before the development had been finished. Then, sales got quiet coming into the new year.

I was still finishing landscaping by the summer of 2020 and putting on the finishing touches for the project. Unfortunately, we were in the middle of the pandemic, and fear plummeted housing and land sales. At this point, I was wholly invested in this venture. What I had earned in the buyout of my shares with my former company was re-invested into the land development. I would have been devastated had I not been able to pull my money back out.

Leading up to this, in 2017, I sold my 20% stake in a company that I had shared ownership in. The buyout was phased over the course of 5 years and was supposed to be for a net amount of $1,600,000. The company's partners needed to secure a financing partner in 2019 and asked me to decrease my buyout to half a million less, so they could increase their share and liquidity position. Being that I am a sympathetic person, I agreed. In exchange, they decided to pay the remainder of the buyout in one lump sum. I agreed to the decreased amount to be compassionate, but fear was also there. I accepted their reduced amount because I feared they would stop paying on the note. If insolvency issues arose, then I would not receive any of the remainder of my buyout. Was it inarguably a great decision? No, but we live and learn. The company probably averages between 70-90 million in sales annually now and continues to grow. But fear is a genuine thing, and when you are leveraged and providing for your family, you may find yourself settling for fear. I hated myself after this. It stole my faith, and I felt like I had made the wrong decision. I accepted fear over courage.

Why do I share this? Because this was where fear began to find its foothold. I am sure I could go further back into my childhood in addressing roots, but this is not a book on psychology, and for the sake of brevity, I will say it materialized there. I didn't realize it then, though. In fact, after the parcel sold in November of that year, and even with the half-million-dollar loss, I still had an excellent year in earnings and was measuring myself by what I had made at that point. So sometime after 2019, and somewhere into 2020, I decided to write this book and start my foundation. But as 2020 lingered, after the summer and into the fall, fear became an ever-growing partner. I remembered that I had just lost half a million dollars the year before. We were also at the height of a growing pandemic that was crippling the world with fear, and it was the perfect storm. This was the beginning of my not believing in the businesswoman I knew I was. When all of your worth is appraised by what you do, your worth and value will be measured by your success. I began to doubt myself.

By October of that year, I decided to sell the development as a whole. Typically, in the region I was developing in, it would generally take 3-5 years to sell a development of that size. I had sold one lot before the development was even finished. It was a testament to the quality of the development. But I didn't even give it a fighting chance. I purchased back the lot I had sold and began to market the entire project. I received three offers in one week and was able to negotiate up to the price point I had wanted.

Shortly after 2021 came in, the market boomed. Individual lot sales went through the roof. I was emailed and called regularly to show the already sold lots. If I had just waited a few more months or so, I could have sold more lots, which would have given me more time, and potentially make a more than 100% return on my investment. If I had just believed in myself... but I was driven by fear at that point.

What I didn't share was that a great deal had gone on before I sold the development. After selling one of the lots, I reached out to a banker for a cap-rate project I was looking at. I needed a financing partner for it. So, I set up the meeting and met with that banker. I pitched my project and then waited for him to review things internally. In between, I called the owner of the bank, who accidentally answered but was unaware that he had.

I listened to him misogynistically trash-talk me for a bit before realizing he was unaware of my being on the other line.

At this point, I hung up. I clearly wasn't going to receive any of their funding for the project I was pitching. By the way, they held several portfolios of land developments. So they were in essence, competitors themselves, with priority given to their portfolio of clients. This, of course, I understood. After all, again, *"business is business."* However, that was still a difficult conversation for me to hear.

There I was, an Asian American Woman, in a predominantly Caucasian city where *"we"* just don't do that type of business. It was a cutting-edge modern development that was very much so against their status quo and ahead of the times. At that point, I began to believe in the lies he spewed about me. I honestly did feel like I was crashing into a glass ceiling that I wasn't interested in breaking anymore and certainly wasn't invited to do so. I won't even tell you what he said on that phone call. You would be horrified...

I didn't realize it because I was still running so fast, but that conversation would later come to haunt me without me ever knowing it. And it wasn't that I hadn't heard worse because, trust me, I had heard much worse. It was just coming from a long season, and I had no more gas to fuel myself. I wasn't getting poured into. I was only pouring out, and when you run on empty, you will eventually run out of gas, and broken down on the side of the highway.

Well, I started with Cinderella and felt it's only appropriate to share that I kept it classy. I also kept *"business, business,"* which is vital to do. Never allow your emotions to get the best of you. It is always perceived as weak, even if the other party you are dealing with is a complete Jack *SS. Women do not need to offer any reason to be perceived as overly emotional and irrational. So, what did I do? I emailed him back. Yes, I did, and this is what I had to say,

Good Afternoon XXXXX,

Thank you for your time earlier. I appreciate you having taken the time out of your day to discuss banking needs. I called a little bit ago and overheard part of your conversation with someone discussing me, perhaps, not in the best of ways. As soon as I realized, I hung up, as not to intrude. I realize the ceiling that I am up against and am in an arena that is dominated by many egos. I am constantly overcoming what people say about me… it comes with the territory, and I am used to it… have been my whole life. If you do not think it's a good fit, please let me know, and I will pursue another route. I need my partnerships to believe in me. However, if so, please send me the needed information with the personal financial disclosure, and I will fill it out along with the tax information. Again, I appreciate your time. Please keep the info provided as sensitive financial information.

Mahalo,

Sarah McFarland

Because, in the end, class does matter. Like Cinderella, if she were to have responded with the same filth that the ugly stepsisters had, Cinderella would not have become the beloved character she is today and may not have inspired so many women as she now does. Despite her circumstances, she prevailed and overcame seemingly difficult odds. Have I always responded as Cinderella would have? Oh, Gosh no…. but that doesn't stop me from trying!

Does it matter if you haven't always taken the most honorable or classiest route in your life? Of course not. No judging here. Look, I grew up in the '90s. In fact, there isn't a whole lot of anything that I haven't done, and no one came out of that era unscathed. We all have had our not-so-proud moments, and that's ok. And if your past tries to follow you, just tell the truth and say what I say, "Well, I'm a big girl now, and I grew up." There honestly isn't much to say after that. Your past only defines you if you let it. How you may have acted before does not set the standard of how you should act going forward. So, set the bar high and bring others up with you, and as I said, your past mistakes don't define your future. They are your mistakes, not their's. So own them.

Selma Hayek stated, *"Even if it's a mistake, it belongs to you. It's yours. Own it. "Yes. I did it." Throw it back in their face, and don't let them take your mistake. Your mistake? It's a valuable tool for growth and for life. Don't be afraid to make mistakes. It's better than to do nothing and learn nothing and not evolve. Your mistake? It's your greatest opportunity and if somebody's making fun of you because you made a mistake, don't go down because of it. If you say, "so what," to their face. If you say, "yes, so what." They are powerless. They are powerless. "Yes, I messed up. Tomorrow it will be another day. Next year will be another year. It is my mistake. Not yours."*

So, "so what to your mistakes," and don't go down with them. Woman evolve.

Well, that banker XXXXX, did end up replying with an apology. He also offered to look at partnering with my development and purchasing it from the other bank. This would have given me time to wait out the negative effects of Covid on the housing market, with the equity it currently had. I did, however, graciously decline. At this point, the letter was more of a formality with the understanding that I had heard his not-so-nice comments. Maybe, if I pointed them out to him, he would pivot and become a better human being. Ultimately, a partnership with him would have been a disaster because he didn't believe in me.

I later realized that moment was a blockage for me, and that I needed to forgive him. I also needed to forgive myself for believing those lies and not having courage. If I had the courage and believed in my value, I may not have sold my shares at a loss. If I had the courage and believed in my value, I also would not have sold the development without seeing my dream come to pass.

Whatever has held you up, it's time to move forward! If it's a person, it's time to forgive them and yourself for allowing their words or actions to delay you. If past mistakes you made are holding you up, forgive yourself and give the younger you some grace. If it's a tragedy, allow yourself to grieve and let the loss be buried. If something was stolen from you, fight to get it back. Get your victory, so you can know that you can win! If it's an internal dialogue, stop partnering with the lies. Find the root and pull it out. If there are labels that say you are who you are not, cast them aside. If fear is holding you back, it's time to believe in yourself! Be free from whatever it is, so you can move forward and blossom, build your empire, and change the world! It's not too late to make an impact and do great things. Don't accept your station in life if you aren't happy with it. If you fell, get back up. The fall already happened. Now that you know why, stop holding on to those reasons and be healed from it. Getting back up is a choice. Choose you! Have courage, Sis, and be kind to the most important person... You!

Chapter 4

LOSING CONTROL

COVID WAS ONE OF THE MOST CHALLENGING TIMES OUR younger generations have ever seen. Everything came to a screeching halt. It was as if the world itself knew that it just needed some time to heal. The pause brought about a re-evaluation and a refocus on life. Many people realized that their lives were severely out of balance. The break took away the busyness, and where some may have once run to things before, they were forced to stop running and just be still. Restaurants shut down. Travel became restricted. People lost their livelihoods and were forced to adapt. Families had to bury their loved ones. Parents had to home-school their children. Social calendars were canceled. People were required to pivot, and fear gripped the world.

The stillness made us all evaluate who we were as individuals. We had to spend time with ourselves, not the distractions that once filled our lives. The quiet made people deal with who they were, and the pandemic allowed you to get to know yourself a little better. You also had more personal time amid a very challenging era. For many people, it was the first time they were mandated on this journey to get to know themselves better. Some people found out that if they were honest, they didn't like themselves as much as they initially thought. Covid allowed us to be stripped down, bare, and without the cover of the world.

Post Covid, mental illness continues to plague our generation. According to Mental Health America's article, "Mental Health and Covid 19," mental illness continues to rise. In comparing multi-response online mental health screenings from 2019 to 2021, a 500% increase occurred. In a health screening that was done in 2021, when those who were screened were asked what they thought the top three things were contributing to their mental health, the respondents answered as follows; 63% reported that one of the top three things contributing to their mental health was loneliness and isolation, 49% reported past trauma and 37% reported relationship problems.

This means that for over half of those screened, being alone was one of the top things that attributed to their mental illness. This suggests that people didn't like being by themselves during that period. I would infer from it that people didn't like themselves as much, either. If you are going to cheerlead yourself, you are going to need to like yourself. You will need to be able to live with who you are and believe in who you are cheering for. This means you will need to like who you are, when no one is around and without anything to hide behind.

Self-love is such an important concept. Not the type of self-love that preens itself in a narcissistic way with IG posts and tic-tok videos delivered by the minute, but a healthy self-love that helps you to love yourself enough so that you don't go the co-dependent way either. An unhealthy narcissistic love always turns inward and atrophies. But, the remarkable thing about healthy love is that it grows, expands, and brings love to an ever-increasing circle whose lives are enriched and nourished by it. Love grows. If you can love who you are, you will most likely love those around you with an even greater love.

When you don't like who you are, you will start to look at the world as a cup a little less full. You have to fight for it to be half full and not settle for the cup half empty. The world is a dark place, but that doesn't mean you have to be dark with it. Be a light in these places. If it's dim, bring a flashlight. A little light will help you get through the darkest of situations! And, as they say, "After the darkest of nights, always comes the dawn." It's inevitable. The light will always pierce through, and if you bring a light, you don't know who else might find their way out as a result of you bringing yours. It starts with you, and the impact is immeasurable. Love yourself enough. Loving who you are will help you to fight for what you will become.

After my divorce, I left my home in Hawaii, remarried, and moved to the Midwest in 2018 with my husband. His family has a mid-size manufacturing company there, and we moved for him to be closer to them so he could help with the business. That is also where I picked up my land development project. I finished the majority of it by the Spring of 2020 and just had landscaping that needed to be completed, which was finalized that summer. I needed a break from a massive project that I had been working on for the past two years, which was long overdue.

I felt overwhelmed by Covid and the division that was happening in the world, and I didn't quite know how to process it all. This was at the height of the pandemic, in the summer of 2020. This was also on the heels of a challenging time for our country following the fatal shooting of Breonna Taylor in Louisville, Kentucky, and Georg Floyd's death in Minneapolis, Minnesota. It was a chilling moment in our history, where I felt the last words of George Floyd, "I Can't Breathe," were indicative of a more outstanding systemic issue within our country. At that moment, I felt as though my very breath had been taken away. I felt it was the culmination of everything we were going through as a country together, and we just couldn't breathe. We just couldn't find our voice.

Overnight, we were locked in, shut down, masked up, and controlled in every facet of our lives. It was a breeding ground for division and anger, and was all just too much to process. People handle tragedy and complex moments in life differently. I needed answers. I hated seeing the America I love so much in its divided state. I needed to understand why it was divided. I needed to come outside of my world to understand someone else's, in the hope it would give me answers to my own questions. I couldn't accept that it was "this opinion" versus that. I wanted to see, on the ground level, why this country was so broken because, genuinely, it did break my heart. I grieved in a great way for the restoration of our country.

What I didn't want to do, was to go on this journey unchanged and full of my own opinions for the sake of someone else's. We far too often discount opinions that are not ours, which is why we end up so divided and broken. I didn't want to be closed-minded to the reality that our country was in deep pain and that it too, *just needed to breathe.* At that time, I didn't realize that this was just the beginning of a journey that would bring me to you. However, it would take years to complete and more complex places to explore. I call this "My Wilderness Season."

At the end of May 2020, my family and I set out on a road trip. I never had the opportunity to be so "irresponsible" and *wild,* and I couldn't wait. We sold our house, let the contractor finish the landscaping on the project, and let the marketing team, do their jobs and sell the development. It was a stagnant time, so not much was moving, and it wasn't going to move with me babysitting it. It was an excellent time to go on a journey of rediscovering ourselves. It was my journey of undoing life and finding faith.

Up until this point, my life was a calendar, with a set of tasks to be completed, followed by future appointments. I lived life as one extensive to-do list. I was always responsible, always prudent, always working and I *just needed to breathe.* I needed to break free of the monotonous routine of work. The pandemic gave me the ability to do so. There is always good to be found, even in "the bad." I also needed to get to know who I was on a deeper level… so I could love who I was on that deeper level. I had never really gotten to explore that version of me.

I got so serious, so young in life, and just pursued the perfect career, family, white picket fence, and picture-perfect postcard. I had, what I thought the picture-perfect life was supposed to look like. I was also constantly moving from one thing to the next and didn't ever have a chance to catch up. This break in life would be that much-needed gift to me. This journey would be many things, but most of all, it would be healing and teach me that there was so much more to me than whether I got an "applause" or a shut door in my face.

We bought a 4x4 Sprinter Van in March 2020. We built it out in two months while simultaneously packing and selling our house. We packed up our Keiki (kids in Hawaiian) and Lani, our standard poodle, and just left. I had no road map, no plans, and no hotels reserved. I had absolutely no idea where we were going, and it was the most incredible feeling in my life! I lost every form of control and found myself in "the wild" that summer of 2020. Imagine, I had no plan for the children's schooling the following year, and I sold my house without knowing where I would go and was technically as homeless as I would ever get. It was reckless, and I was reveling in anticipation. I wanted to live in a van and not be tied down to the world and just go, even if it was only for the summer. This is coming from a country club, Louboutin-wearing, Louis Vuitton-toting, kind of girl. And I wasn't always her.

As a child, I was wild. I was in the rivers, mountain biking everywhere, clearing jumps in the forest, and coming home with scars on my face that would leave my mother speechless and in tears. In a sense, at this moment, I was permitting myself to be that kid again. I was allowing *myself* to go and break the rules a little and not have a plan all the time. Losing control was the healthiest thing I had ever done for myself, and I didn't ask for permission to do it. I just did it! Losing control is where I found who I was. I asked God, at that moment, to meet me in the wilderness of life and to direct the journey. I needed to find inner peace again, away from my life's obligations. My therapist told me, "Sarah, you live on the edge, and you need to have some *wild* from time to time to feel alive." I think we all need that "wild" at times. Something in us sleeps until a time of change or transition. I believe we are made with the innate desire for the changing of seasons, both in nature and in our lives. So, we need uncertainty at times. Transcending moments can come from unplanned, wild, and unruly seasons.

So, the rebel in me was loosed, and I was as free as I had ever felt, and this was my great F…U… moment! This was my great unraveling, my glorious undoing. The finding of who I was and was called to be, and I went for it! I distinctly remember my Mother-in-Law asking my husband right before we started the van, "Patrick, are you just going to be ok with not knowing where you are going to go?" And we 100% were! I found myself that summer of 2020, and it may have been a little late at 35, but better late than never.

We traversed the West Coast to the East Coast and then returned to the West Coast again. We explored the Rocky Mountains, the Appalachian Mountains, the Smokey Mountains, and the Mountains of the Sonoran Desert. We were surrounded and awakened by the police twice, got stuck in the sand, and hauled out from a beach. We swam with the beavers while jumping into ice-cold aquifers and slept where mountain lions and coyotes roamed. We explored an America that we had never seen. We went to the small towns of Tennessee and saw the kind and hardworking Americans, the backbone of this country, continue to work through a difficult time.

We also saw Colorado's mining and casino towns, where not one person could be seen, and where the effects of the pandemic had left those places utterly decimated and desolate. It was as though we were walking through an apocalyptic movie at times. Lights lit up and down a street with casinos, with no car in sight. The music continued to play, from each small casino and restaurant, waiting for the visitors that never came. It was haunting and surreal. We had the unique ability to see how every town, county, and state walked through Covid. Each was very different, and we saw how it impacted the people living in those towns and counties.

We drove through the cities of Louisville and St Louis because we wanted to understand the moment we were living in. So we rode through history that summer. Streets were shattered with glass. Boards took the place of windows. Looting was rampant, and communities were seemingly segregated. The nation was in pain, and it was visible on every street and on every corner. The country was divided, and *just needed to breathe.*

It was from that moment that "Let Love Be Greater" was born. I had found a "Why." I saw that ignoring a hurting country would never heal the sins of its past, and what we had seen that summer was the built-up pain, anger, and frustration of Americans, who felt like they couldn't breathe who had lost their voice. At that moment, a seed was planted in me. It wouldn't take root for some time until later, but the seed of wanting to bring hope to a broken world was sown. Mother Teresa famously stated, "Spread love everywhere you go. Let no one ever come to you without leaving happier." Indeed, she made the world a better place.

I found a passion on that trip. Later, I would put the framework together for this vision. I wanted to build a foundation that would be the bridge to a broken world. What resonated with me was to help women in need of a second start in life. The organization would focus on bridging the gap by offering scholarships and aid to women at an economic and socio-economic disadvantage. I began to find worth beyond just my own personal value as an entrepreneur. I began to think outside of who I was and who I wanted to be, and that version of me was someone I could grow to be proud of and really like. I began to dream!

Chapter 5

SELF-FULFILLING PROPHECY

Well, it's chapter 5, and I am still here! Are you getting up with me? Are we doing this together? Have you been challenging yourself to go deeper? Have you found the courage to receive that healing, find your identity and love yourself yet! I am proud of myself, and you should be proud of yourself too. I came back to you, and you are still reading! Take the wins. You have already accounted for the losses. Now take the victories too! Remember to be good to yourself. Remember to *love* yourself. Start seeing the cup half-full. You have to fight to keep it there! It's a daily walk, not just something you think of occasionally. Seldom, won't get you off your bed and out of your house. Seldom…won't fight for you when you are so exhausted you feel mentally paralyzed and can't seem to move. This is every day! Every day, encourage yourself! Every day, appreciate who you are. Every day, thank yourself for being here because you are choosing to fight for *yourself* and not give up! You are reading a book on *getting up*, which means you want to get up! You may not know how to, and that's ok. You are on the path toward that goal and are putting in some valuable time and effort to change the direction of your life. Just pause, meditate on that for a while, and give yourself some credit!

I have a girlfriend who is dear to me. We went through a challenging time at similar moments in our lives. We experienced a great deal of loss together. We took our kids on a trip during our friendship, and I remember seeing her carry around this little jar. Every night, she would write something and put it in the jar. I asked her what it was, and she said it was her "grateful jar." She said she would write out what she was grateful for and put it in that jar nightly. That profoundly impacted me. She was going through the most difficult season of her life then, and still fought to keep her jar *half full*…. literally. She fought for her joy, and that was a choice. She had a grateful heart in the middle of tragedy and believed she would see better days ahead, and she did.

I believe our words and belief systems have a lot of power. We give life or death to the circumstances and situations in our world. We can change how we think with so little as a "grateful jar" and use those reminders to keep our heads above water and turn a negative situation into a very positive one. I believe that what we say can directly impact our outcome at times, and how we think matters. In social psychology, this is called the "self-fulfilling prophecy."

Wikipedia defines it as "*something that comes true at least in part as a result of a person's or group of persons' belief or expectation that* said prediction would come true. This suggests that people's beliefs influence their actions. The principle behind this phenomenon is that people create consequences regarding people or events, based on previous knowledge of the subject."

The Encyclopedia Britannica defines it as "an individual's expectations about another person or entity eventually result in the other person or entity acting in ways that confirm the expectations."

To put this into practice, the article "The truth behind a self-fulfilling prophecy" from the Cleveland Clinic shares, "Self-fulfilling prophecies are a complex phenomenon that involves multiple psychological layers," states Dr. Albers. "When you set certain expectations, those expectations can lead you to notice certain things but not pay attention to others. Your mind focuses on details that confirm what you expect.

This is especially true when it comes to your medical care. One easy example of this is the placebo effect. This phenomenon occurs when a person participating in a clinical trial experiences improvement in their condition even though they received sugar pills or saline and water injections instead of an actual treatment.

Although the exact mechanism that causes the placebo effect is not known, doctors believe the physical changes in your body occur as a result of your brain releasing a series of certain hormones in response to your belief that you're receiving real treatment.

"It shows the power of the mind and belief. Your body doesn't distinguish between what is true and false. It only needs to believe something is true to respond as if it is," explains Dr. Albers. "The saying 'It's all in your head,' has some merit. If you tell yourself, 'I'm not doing well,' your body is listening. Your mind will send signals to *your body and release chemicals that support this notion, like stress chemicals and an immune response."*

Self-fulfilling prophecies play out in medical outcomes, patient satisfaction and your overall health and well-being, too."

As shown here by Dr. Albers, this would suggest that our thought patterns and what we think of ourselves or our situations can impact the very direction of that outcome. Simply put, If you believe you are a loser, you will be a loser. If you think you are a winner, you will be a winner! I believe we will change our outcomes if we can change how we think about ourselves. I choose to have faith over fear. I choose to love myself and believe in who I am. I will finish that product line, create that invention, buy that company, and write that book.... You fill in the blank. These are all powerful words, and what you say about yourself will impact what you do. So, agree to give yourself the best version of who you are and partner with who you want to become! What have you been saying that does not agree and align with where you are going and who you want to be? It's as simple as changing your mindset. Stop spewing out the negative and start adopting the positive. The battlefield truly is in the mind. What do you want to say about your situation? Who do you want to be? Now speak the words that feed that vision and get your mind to believe in yourself!

In 2017, I was diagnosed with Asperger's. Asperger's is a level of being on the spectrum. I like to use the words, Spectric. Eccentric and the word spectrum combined! The Asperger's Foundation describes Asperger's Syndrome as *"a pervasive developmental condition that falls within the autistic spectrum. Autism is a lifelong developmental disability that affects how a person communicates with and relates to other people as well as how they experience the world around them. Asperger's Syndrome is sometimes referred to as High Functioning Autism (HFA) or Autism Spectrum Condition (ASC). It can affect people of all genders and ages within all cultural and social environments.*

The condition is characterized by difficulties with social interaction, social communication and flexibility of thinking or imagination. In addition, there may be sensory, motor and organizational difficulties. The condition was first identified over 50 years ago by Hans Asperger, a Viennese pediatrician.

A pattern of behaviors and abilities was identified, predominantly amongst boys, including a lack of empathy, impaired imagination, difficulty in making friends, intense absorption in special interests and often problems with motor co-ordination."

Asperger's is how your brain processes how you think, and how you respond may be a little unique. Some people have no idea what having Aspergers means, so they unintentionally try to categorize it. It is how your mind was created to operate and think. It is outside of the norm. So, the world is still adjusting and finding a box to put it into. But sometimes, there is no box, and sometimes there is no proper label, and it is just another creative way we were made to think.

If we all thought the same, life would be dull and unimaginative. And yes, I do look people in the eye, can hold conversations, have a social life, and care deeply for people. Many people don't know that women with Asperger's are often misdiagnosed and underdiagnosed. Women tend to mask what they perceive as their weaknesses and inadequacies much better than men. I didn't realize how my brain worked until later in life, and I always felt odd and out of the box. I felt like I could never find a place to fit in, so growing up was extremely difficult for me. I made a lot of wrong decisions just trying to fit in. I was also unable to discern people's intentions as well, and was therefore more easily taken advantage of. I had to learn how to navigate through overcoming the difficulties I faced.

I ended up going to college for a Marketing Communications Degree. I had no idea, at that point, how valuable that would be to me later in life. College helped me tremendously to learn how to communicate and communicate well. A perceived weakness became a strength by unknowingly tackling the area of my life where I was weakest in. After school, I began working in politics, hosted fundraisers, emceed events, and hosted a small local tv show for those elected officials I worked for. All of this was before the age of 22 and long before my diagnosis. My relationships and social standing played to my strengths with a girl that always had the same condition. My mind was unwilling to be a victim, even though it never even knew my diagnosis until later. There were challenges, but unknowingly, my mind chose to overcome them.

It was a sigh of relief when I learned about my diagnosis. I always knew that I was different, but I didn't know why. Instead of covering it up, being ashamed, and thinking there was something wrong with me, I embraced the newfound information. I began to research, study and understand how my mind worked. This helped me to put a lot of missing pieces to the puzzle together and also helped me learn how to work with my weaknesses. I began to see where the pitfalls were in my former marriage, where I had difficulty in transitioning to new things, and where I could improve upon them in my new one.

I also saw the strengths and began to focus on those too. Aspergers comes with the ability to hyper-focus on something with such force that it could take me weeks what might take someone a year to do, and likewise, if things are out of place in my world, it could take me a year or more, in what should have only taken weeks for someone else to do. I focused on creating an environment that prevented my weaknesses from overcoming me. I worked around them and got help where I needed it. If the house was messy and I knew I couldn't function because of some extreme OCD, I got a cleaner to come regularly and help with that. If I knew I would be over-stimulated with having functions and obligations all week, I would make time for some spa and yoga therapy the following week. If I knew I couldn't move on to the next project until what I was working on was 100% done, I would enlist help from someone to get it done. I stopped hating and fighting my weaknesses. Instead, I worked through and around them. I worked with my strengths and strengthened them, and allowed my creativity to take on new roles.

I also often get bored if I do the same thing repeatedly. It's just how my mind was created. Although I thrive in routine, I also enjoy being challenged. So rather than allow it to be a negative, I look for new areas I want to learn about and either invest or work in them. I use the need to be challenged and stimulated to constantly find novel areas of engagement and enjoy being a lifelong learner.

In this regard, I learned about my diagnosis and chose not to be a victim of it. Instead, I asked myself, "Who do I say that I am, and what do I say that I am capable of?" The diagnosis would be what I allowed it to be, and all I allowed it to be, was a piece of the puzzle that would help me to understand who I was better. I did not allow it to handicap me.

Labels can be used to help you understand certain things better, and aren't all horrible. At the same time, many can also be used to hurt you. My son was having a difficult time in school when he was younger. He had a hard time sitting still and would often lose focus. His teacher was adamant that there was something wrong with him. I got the "In 25 years… I have never seen such a child" talk. This was a problematic assessment for me to understand. My son was a reasonably well-behaved boy. He just didn't like to sit for long periods of time. What five year old does? But he was kind to his peers, never hit anyone, and always said thank you. She was indignant that Reagan had ADHD. Well, I was indignant that he didn't. I took him to the best Psychiatrist on the Island for a behavioral diagnosis, where he underwent five days of observations, testing, and Psychiatric evaluations.

At the end of it, the Psychiatrist told me that my son was a genius, smarter than 99% of the children he would be around, and that he was just bored out of his mind. Now, I went back to the teacher with his full report done by the best clinic, the one they had recommended, and when I handed it to her, she was baffled. She had placed upon my son at the age of five a label that I was not willing to give him, and because I didn't partner with it and stand for that truth, I stopped him from receiving a label that was not true to who he was. Now I am not saying that ADHD isn't real or is bad because it is real, and it isn't bad. I am saying that it wasn't *his reality,* and I wasn't about to put him on medicine when he didn't need it. Every day, I tell my children that they are smart, kind, and beautiful, and they are. Every day, I encourage them so that my words will fight back against this world's unnecessary labels and thought patterns. What we say matters. What we think matters.

The world will put you in a box if you let it. It's looking to categorize you from the day you are born. Don't allow someone else's label that isn't true. What labels do you need to re-assess and work with versus work against? What labels simply need to be peeled off and thrown out? There is a difference. Begin to differentiate them in your life and start speaking the self-fulfilling prophecy that you want to come to pass.

Chapter 6

PURPOSE DRIVEN: FINDING YOUR WHY?

M ARK TWAIN ONCE STATED, "THE TWO MOST IMPORTANT days in your life are the day you are born and the day you find out why." So, why were you born? If you ask this question and allow yourself to think about it earnestly, you may find that you do not know why, and to find the answer, you will need to go on a deeper journey. You may learn that being successful and climbing the corporate ladder probably won't be the answer either. What happens when you climb it? Then what? If you are looking for just a title, accomplishments, and a position in life, what happens when you get that too? Or perhaps, what happens when you don't get it? If your world revolves around being President of the Ferrari club, what happens when you can't afford your Ferrari or get replaced with the next up-and-coming fad? If your purpose revolves around work, what happens when you retire or get fired? If it's the local ministry at your church, what happens if you move or if they disappoint you?

Is your "why" to be a mom? If everything revolves around your children and being a mom, what happens when the kids grow up? Who are you without them? What's the purpose of producing another generation? What's the fulfillment? Love? Ok, then, what happens if you get divorced? This doesn't mean that you don't get some meaning and fulfillment from these things, but if all your meaning is the summation of other people and things, then don't be surprised if your "Why" gets stolen sometimes. And then, what becomes of your identity or your calling? You can't depend on others or things to give you reasons for your entire existence.

When you are 80 years old, alone or not, looking back, what will be the most significant accomplishments that bring you the most gratification? Life is deeper than a Ferrari or a corner office. Lean too far on them, and you will eventually be left disappointed and empty. What will bring you the most joy and value, even if you are on your own? If Mother Theresa found her only value in life was to be married, she would have never changed the world. Her "Why" was to make this world a better place, and it had nothing to do with the children she had or did not have because she didn't have any. She chose a much larger cause than what was reflected in her immediate surroundings. She *chose* the orphans of the world to impact and find purpose with. She believed in what she was doing and went beyond her own self-satisfaction, consideration, or even personal remuneration.

If Princess Diana had settled only to be a princess, she would have never revolutionized how we see AIDS. She brought compassion into a very controversial and stigmatized disease and broke the barriers and misconceptions surrounding it. She was considered one of the greatest humanitarians of our time, and it didn't stop just because she got a divorce. She used her platform as a princess to reach some of the world's most impoverished nations. Princess Diana didn't work to seek her title. She used her title to seek her purpose. So, what is your *purpose*? What is your "*why*?" I can't answer that. No one can answer that but you. Only you can, and that answer will be different for everyone because we are all called to do different things in life. But I implore you to go deeper than the surface level of what you do, who you are, or even the immediate vicinity that you operate in. I implore you to go outside of yourself to find this question.

For some, fulfillment may look like their impact on their legacy and the world they leave behind. For others, it may be to change the world in the spheres of influence they are called to. And wherever you find joy and fulfillment, most likely, you will find your purpose. For me? I am still finding purpose every day, but every day, I get a little closer to knowing who I am and what I was born to do. It's a journey and is never entirely perfected. Passions can evolve, and people still find purpose in their later years too. Purpose can be lifelong or, for a season in our lives, to be replaced when they are fulfilled.

My passion is to help others come up. I receive joy and fulfillment to some regard in my family...yes; and in my marriage...yes; and in the work that I do... yes. But a greater joy and fulfillment come from what I do, to help heal this world and make it a better place for future generations. And I don't have to tackle it all. I just do what I can in the spheres of influence that I have. So many people have helped to pick me up. So, when I see someone down, I believe in paying it forward. Get picked up, pick one up. Get helped up. Help one up. Mother Teresa also said, "If you can't feed the world, feed one." So, if helping others is your passion, start with one. Eventually, you will get to the point where there will be many coming up with you, and your good deeds will go viral.

The first thing I ever did with my foundation was to pay for a woman's down payment on her apartment lease. Did it change the world? No. But did it change her life? Yes. That woman was in an abusive relationship and had no money to get out of it. It is a travesty in our society that money is sometimes the only thing that stands in the way of a woman being physically beaten or finding her freedom. That down payment allowed her to get out of a dangerous situation at the time, and I was able to impact this particular sphere of her life. Again, it's the little things. Famous American basketball coach and player John Robert Wooden said, "It's the little details that are vital. Little things make big things happen." Mr. Wooden won ten National Collegiate Athletic Association Championships as head coach for the UCLA Bruins within 12 years. The woman I helped went on to get married to a lovely man and is now free from the cycle of physical and emotional abuse. Who knows what great things her future will hold!

Your "Why" should be the very reason you want to work. Another "Why" for me is my *legacy*. It is what I will leave behind for future generations. It goes beyond wanting to raise my two children. It is the legacy I will leave for my children's children and the impact I will have on the generations to come, notwithstanding only mine. What I do now impacts how my children will live, and if you don't have children or want children, that is ok too. What you do now will still influence how the world will live long after you are gone. Some of the most dynamic and impactful women we have seen in our generation do not have children.

Oprah Winfrey never had children, which did not stop her from using her billions to make the world a better place and help the less fortunate. Yue Sai Kan, dubbed the "Oprah of China," likewise did not have children, and her impact on Chinese American relations is invaluable. People Magazine called her "The most famous person in China." Time Magazine called her "The Queen of the Middle Kingdom." She helped to usher in a new era for the women of China by introducing makeup there. She built her empire by bringing them self-confidence and beauty.

Building a makeup empire was what Yue Sai did to create her wealth. What she did with her wealth, and continues to do now, is increase political relations between China and America. Inarguably, there has never been a more valuable time than today for such a need within our current geopolitical state. She also helps to bring Chinese culture to the world and fundraises for various organizations. She has now transitioned into being a world-famous humanitarian. Yue Sai took her platform as a Chinese Fashion Icon and Emmy Award-Winning Host and Producer and used it to launch herself as the ambassador for championing women through her charity work. Through her humanitarian work, she has pioneered, in a significant way, to empower and bring beauty to women worldwide. Her impact will be seen past her generation and the generations to come. Both Oprah and Yue Sai will leave an incredible legacy behind.

What is your legacy? What do you want to leave behind? What brings you joy and fulfillment when you do it? What does your heart have compassion for? *Purpose* will give you the drive to work and the desire to supply that need.

Your circumstances do not determine your outcome. Your lousy moment does not limit your purpose or what you are capable of doing! Some of the most extraordinary beauty and passion were birthed during the most painful moments of my life. In 2016, I was going through a profoundly challenging divorce. I remember not knowing how I would ever get back up from that moment. I was going through something that I could not control and did not have a choice in, and not knowing and not having control was perhaps the most difficult part. No one had ever been divorced in my direct family line before. I was a first. If you know about being on the spectrum, divorce and a change like that are extremely difficult to bounce back from.

A piece of my puzzle had just been lost. No matter how hard I tried to find it, the piece was nowhere to be found. I had lost my routine, so I did not know what to do next or how to move forward. I don't know how I got through that time in my life other than by the grace of God. I had no will to survive or desire even to be a mother. Had it not been for my children, I'm unsure if I would be here to write this book. But I remembered thinking I could not leave this world without seeing my children healthy, happy, and whole. If it were the last thing I ever did, I would fight for them. At that point, the purpose I found in them was enough to get me to live. The only thing I could do was hold on to that because I didn't have anything else. I wasn't able to dream. I just needed to survive.

People don't just commit suicide because they are weak and selfish. I abhor that assumption. Sometimes they just think the world would be better off without them, and often, they can't see any way forward. Suicide is a deeply painful thing to contemplate, and if you are at that moment right now, please let me encourage you… there is hope on the other side of you getting back up, and this world desperately needs to see you get back up! Suicide is a permanent solution to what is only a temporary albeit excruciating problem. If you can push past this moment, you will see hope on the other side. So, fight through today because tomorrow will come!

I believe the most beautiful people have walked through some of the most harrowing tragedies. They have seen loss, heartbreak, and loneliness. When they overcome, they will carry the keys to unlock those same doors they see shut on others. They will bring freedom to those around them. When you have walked through something, you can recognize it in others walking through it. Your heart that sees that will be the heart used to heal this world! Your ability to empathize and have compassion for those who are hurting is needed to bring value and love to others around you. I have often seen that some of the happiest-looking people are the saddest inside. They have far too much compassion to break down those around them, so a smile is brought wherever they go. They know what it is like to live with so much sadness. They smile and make you laugh while their light is slowly dimming. If that's you, remember, it is always darkest before the dawn… and the dawn must and always will follow.

So if this *is* you, please choose to *fight* for you! Please choose the future you and everything you are called to do and are meant to become. Your value isn't summarized by this moment that has you feeling trapped. Your value is so much more than you could ever imagine, and your getting up will be the light that brings the dawn. There is a treasure on the inside of you waiting to get out. Take that depth of darkness, recognize it others and rescue the people around you! You are more needed, more important, and more valuable than you could ever imagine! People that go through some of the darkest things and make it through, are some of the most valuable and impactful human beings around! So don't sell yourself short right before you get to see some of the most beautiful sunrises come to pass! Light always comes after darkness!

Your worth isn't created by one person and what they say about you. Nor is it about how much money you have in the bank or what you don't have. It's not in the things that you have or the car that you drive. The looming bankruptcy won't break you, the death of a loved one won't paralyze you, and what happened to you in your past can't define you. What's happening to you now doesn't get to stop you. You can't see it, but these opportunities will catapult you into the woman of strength and character you were destined to be. You have a choice. You can allow this moment to either break you or make you. Use all of it. All of what you feel, what you are going through, and all of the pain. Use it to catapult you into the next season of your life! You can either focus on your failures and the things that happened to you, and allow yourself to become the victim, or you can use it to be the driving force behind your will and determination to succeed, get back up, and find greatness!

The same year I was going through a heartbreaking divorce, I also found purpose. I found another "why."

Before I share this next story, I would like first to preface that what I am about to state is from my version of an international dispute, and the truths of it are from my recollection, and there may be other truths to it. By no means am I willing to take the liability and state that there are no other possible deviations from what is shared here.

A small land-locked country in the Middle East has been in dispute for several decades with two of its neighboring countries. It was during the collapse of the Soviet Union that these nations have since disputed it. In 1994, one of the neighboring countries was eventually given control over it as a de facto protectorate. Since then, its other neighbor, a wealthy oil-producing country, has breached several ceasefire agreements. This small, land-locked country is impoverished, with 120,000 inhabitants and virtually no ability to protect itself. There is also no dispute that the inhabitants living there wanted to stay as a de facto protectorate of the originally assigned country, as their heritage closely aligned with theirs. For decades, this small nation has had to deal with fatal shootings from their unruly neighbor on their border.

In 2016, I was asked to help introduce some legislation (resolutions) at Hawaii's city and state levels. At the time, several other states were introducing similar legislation. The legislation recognized this small country as independent, outside of this second country's ownership interests. In a sense, it was saying that we, in America, stand by you, and we see you. I worked hard alongside elected local and state leaders and community members in Hawaii to see this through. I used what I had in that moment and within my sphere of influence to help make an impact.

On March 30, 2016, the Hawaii State House and Senate passed the Resolution. It simultaneously passed out of the Honolulu City Council as well. Shortly after the Resolution had passed, it was rumored that the sitting Secretary of State, had his office reach out and request that the State Senate rescind the recognition and issue an immediate apology, stating that there would be irrevocable effects on international diplomatic relations. At that time, I believe there was something about a mutual benefit with airspace rights in the vicinity, and this did not bode well for our relations or privileges with them.

The Hawaii House and State Senate did not pivot to the administration's requests. Shortly after, on April 1st 2016, just two days after the passage of the Resolution, the 1994 ceasefire agreement was breached once again by the country unwilling to abdicate the desire to control it. Soldiers of this nation decimated the lives of hundreds of their indefensible neighbor. It was later stated to be a retaliation effort by some. However, it was believed that this battle had long been planned for quite some time. The disinformation campaign has been ongoing.

By helping to pass the Resolution, Hawaii helped to bring an international spotlight to the ongoing breaches of a ceasefire agreement between the two nations. It helped shine a light on the constant invasions and bullying of a helpless country land-locked on every side.

President Putin organized a trilateral negotiation shortly after, bringing another temporary ceasefire. As a result, the international community was forced to look at the travesties facing that small nation and intervene. From there, a small country with no voice in the international community found its voice, and people began to hear their cries. In 2017, Hawaii State Congresswoman Tulsi Gabbard championed bettering relations between the nation and their surrounding neighbors. Again, the communities were hearing these countries' lost voices.

I wasn't paid anything, wasn't publicly recognized then, and wasn't given anything to help out. I had no ties whatsoever by blood or relation to these countries. I was willing to see a nation that had lost its voice. When you have lost your own, you can sometimes recognize when others have lost their voice too. And when you can see other people, the purpose gets even larger. Soon you can then see groups, communities, and even nations. You will be put into defining moments in history, and if you can see beyond your circumstance, you will be able to change the course and trajectory of the events surrounding you and those around you. So, don't discount your seemingly invisible moment. You may very well find purpose during the most unexpected times.

Even though I felt like my voice was unheard that season, I still used it to speak up for those who had none. The California State Legislature later recognized me for my humanitarian efforts, and I was given a flag that flew over the United States Capital, by one of our Congressional Members, in recognition of the actions I had put forth that year.

Bring a light to whatever dark place you are at and shine it brightly. The spotlight that you produce may very well impact the world!

Chapter 7

GROWING IN THE DARK

A SPARK WAS LIT AFTER THE SUMMER OF 2020, AND A PURPOSE was born. I was beginning to find myself on this journey of re-discovery. I didn't have all the pieces to the puzzle yet, but I started to step outside of who I thought I was and began to seek who I was called to be. We ended up settling in Arizona, where my family lived. We visited them earlier that summer while on our epic ride cross-country and decided, with quite a bit of impulsivity, Arizona would do. We didn't know how long we would stay, just that it was all part of the journey. We had spent the past two years with Patrick's family. So, I guess it just made sense to spend some time with mine. It was a season of going back to old roots and finding healing through it.

We purchased a home, put the kids in school, and picked up right where we left off. I joined the local country club, got the kids in their extracurricular activities, and started flying back and forth to Nebraska to work on the development. I had a taste of freedom that summer, but when I got settled in, I found myself in the same hustle and bustle. I kept myself busy at work and started the application process for the foundation. When I returned to work on the project, the landscaping was done, and it was magnificent. The development had finally been completed, and it was right on time. We stuck to deadlines, pushed hard to get the things through, and did it. I then checked in with the marketing team, who were tasked with marketing and selling the development, and still, no progress in sales had been made.

Picking your team is vital, and finding people that you can trust and partner with is crucial. Before selecting this team, I had chosen to work with another one, but there were some significant challenges that I will not go into for the sake of not sounding pithy. After I signed the contract with them, several issues began to erupt. I realized quickly that this would put the sales of the development in jeopardy. So, I knew I needed to pivot fast to another team. When made aware, one of the team members got upset, hijacked my Facebook page, and wrote some very damaging words about it. Incredible… First, the banker, then this. I could have sued for damages but chose to rise above it at that moment in time. After moving forward with the new team, we hit a slowdown from Covid 19 and sales were halted. Covid in addition to the damage done from the previous team had put the project in jeopardy.

At this point, I realized stagnation was beginning to settle in. And as I mentioned, it was difficult to sell land during the middle of the pandemic. Fall was approaching, and I wasn't patient enough. I was fearful, and that fear did not bode well. If I had owned the development flat out, I wouldn't have looked at selling, but I had a partner, and that partner was the bank. By the way, the bank was an incredible partnership, and I was very blessed by them and their belief in what I was doing. But at the end of the day, "*business is business*," and they had their deadlines to meet. I had the potential to pull out equity and refinance the loan, but I was tired and didn't believe in me enough. I didn't have any fight left, and I had lost my courage from a busy season of battling.

I decided to sell myself short and sell the development as a whole. When I finally decided to do so, I reached out to some other builders and developers and had three offers within the same week. I settled for good when things could have been great. I sold myself out on my dream because I didn't believe in myself enough. And as I stated earlier, in Chapter 3, 2021 was a record-breaking year for real estate sales nationwide. I missed out on that opportunity because of fear. Never allow fear and not believing in yourself to hold you back from being great. If you can see the finish line, do yourself a favor and get to it! Run, walk, crawl, get carried, be dragged, but whatever you do, get across that finish line! You will thank the younger you in the retelling of your story.

After that sale, I was tired. I made out ok, but it wasn't the home run I was looking for. I stopped writing this book and would put it away for the next three years of my life. I was lost somewhere in the fantastic "Aether" of space and was finally so exhausted that I knew I needed to rest and re-balance. I had lost my passion and didn't have too much of a desire to do anything in business. I was sick with extremely high cholesterol, and my health was in poor condition. I was burned out, and it took me 15 years to get there. So, I just let myself breathe and focused on my physical and mental well-being.

The quiet set in, and I had a lot of time to re-access my values and what was important to me, and that's exactly what I did. *Purpose* was still alive in my soul, but it didn't find a healthy place to be birthed, and I needed to find that place. When pregnant with a baby, you care for yourself and that baby. You eat the right foods and avoid harmful and unsafe conditions because getting that baby to full term is hard work. And then, when the baby is born, you look for a safe place to have that child in.

The birthing time is a dangerous moment. If the conditions aren't right, you could lose your infant and produce a stillborn. Once that baby is born, it becomes completely dependent upon you, which is its most fragile time… in its infancy. You have to feed and nurse that baby with the milk you produce. You've got to protect it while you teach it to crawl, then teach it to walk and talk, and one day, teach that child to be independent and strong enough to go out on its own into the world. So much is the same as with a seed. A seed grows in the dark. It is hidden from the elements and kept safe from the storms. Too much water would root it out. Too much sun would dry it up and never allow it to grow. The soil helps to offer the protection the seed needs until it is strong enough to come out of the ground and face the storms of life. It grows it's roots in the dark and is protected while in the dirt.

And so much can be the same with purpose, as with a seed or a baby. *Purpose,* when planted, is something as small as a seed. It can grow in the dark and be nourished in the dark. As a baby needs protection from the outside world, so does your purpose! Brought out too soon, and it will be premature. Early exposure can kill it. The pregnancy and complete gestational process offers the strength for that baby to survive outside in the world. Share your vision and bring it out too soon, and you could lose your faith and want to abort that vision to the fear and criticisms surrounding you. Without the proper support and maturity, the correct setup, and foundation, that purpose can come out dead if it doesn't have the right environment to protect it.

And when you bring your dream to the birthing room, it is at its most fragile time of life. According to the World Health Organization, "75% of neonatal deaths occur during the first week of life." And if it's a business venture, the odds of making it are against you. According to Lending Tree, 18.4% of private-sector businesses in the U.S. fail within the first year. After five years, 49.7% have faltered, while after ten years, 65.5% of companies have failed. Those are astounding numbers. That means more than half of all businesses will have failed by the tenth year.

You have to feed that dream to keep it alive. You have to protect, care for, and get it strong enough until it can stand on its own. Just like a baby growing in the womb, or a seed growing in the dark, your purpose will need you to guard and nourish it. It will require the strength to withstand what it will have to go up against in the future, and the process of what is done in the dark will provide the maturity to sustain the difficult road ahead. When you grow in the dark, hidden away and allow yourself the entire maturation process, you will know how to hold the flashlight because you know what it's like to need it in dark places.

Don't discount what is done in the dark. Dark places can create incredible growth. Thank God all your prayers weren't answered in the wrong season and at the wrong time! You might have lost the very thing that needed to be birthed out of you. You may not see it, but the rain from the storms you were sheltered from provides the nutrients required to grow your roots down deep. The storms produce rain. Storms are an inevitable cycle of nature to sustain growth. Whether invited or not, they will come. However, when you are underneath the soil growing, you are sheltered from their destructive nature, and yet still receive the rain.

The soil that has kept you in its dark and seemingly lonely environment, offers the right surroundings to mature and grow you. And when your seed grows into a tree and bears fruit, you will have to face the storms. But this time around, they will not uproot your deep system and shake off the fruit you produce in the coming season. No matter how much fruit you have, it will all get stolen when your roots are shallow. The wind and rain will shake your very foundation until all that you produced in former seasons falls to the ground, becomes rotten, and is no more. Sometimes the greatest gift you can give yourself is time. Time to heal, time to learn. Time to get stronger, and time to change. So as one of my best friends stated, "Babygirl, let it rain. Let it rain. Let it rain.... Girl, Let it Rain!"

As I was not in a healthy place then, the foundation's approval came and was received in silence. I had fallen down again, and this time, it was more of a gradual one, more of a gradual settling that slowly took away the desire to fight, and not only could I not get up, I did not want to get up. It was the culmination of running a race, and I had run out of gas. I spent the rest of the children's school year in Arizona and then decided to return to Hawaii in 2021. I had prided myself on the ability to get up. I got up from my divorce. I got up from being pulled down time and time again. I got up with every door slammed in my face. I got up when deals unraveled. I rose to the occasion in business negotiations. I got up when no more women or men were standing in the room. I cheered myself through seemingly impossible circumstances. When one door closed, I kicked the next one open. I had gotten up so many times before, but there was something different about this one. It was a slow fade into a dark time.

I came back to a home I did not recognize. So, I did a complete 360 and ended up right back where I started. The traveling and the unraveling were me losing control of a life that had always controlled me. But as I returned for comfort, what I had known, had become almost entirely unrecognizable. There were shut-down restaurants, weekly Covid tests, major division, political unrest, a slowly deflating economy, people getting fired over vaccine mandates, and fear running rampant throughout the state. It was the worst possible time to come back to Hawaii, but this was my home, and that wasn't going to stop me. The rest of the world was waking up, but Hawaii was starting to go to sleep. I had been able to avoid the effects of Covid to a great degree until this point, and overnight, it became eerily silent.

Hawaii was where I was forced to deal with who I was without everything else that had accompanied me before. I wasn't building my next project, and I wasn't doing anything. The pandemic had put me on pause, and I had nowhere to run. I faced myself and started to answer all of the questions like "Why?" "Who am I?" and "What made me run? What made me drop it?" Where did this passion go? I found a little purpose on my summer trip in 2020, but why couldn't I hold onto it? Why couldn't I finish my book or get the foundation going? Why couldn't I get back out into the world again? I told myself I was prideful and that this patient time would teach me to endure and become humble. That ultimately, this would be good for me, but it was so much more than that. I found myself hating who I was. I felt like I was a weak failure, an imposter, and a coward. I didn't have faith in myself and didn't have the motivation to get back up. I started to get comfortable with not doing, and complacency became me. My identity had been stripped, and I had to find out who I was without a cover. I felt like everything that I was, was a lie... I felt like I had run my drive into the ground, and now I was like a cow being set out to pasture. I had officially retired myself at this moment, and it was all before the age of 40.

This would become a time of resetting my focus and rebuilding my identity. I was finding myself in the unraveling of who I was on this journey. I had to face what I didn't like and rewrite truths about who I was and who I wanted to become. My foundation wasn't strong enough to take me to where I needed to go, and the lies and labels of who the world told me I was, needed to be peeled off. This was just the first time it was quiet enough to face what I was running from, which was inevitably me. I needed to love myself again, believe in my purpose and calling, and believe in what I was doing. I had been carrying around a heavy backpack while climbing up a never-ending mountain, and every time I climbed higher, I picked up another bag. This quiet time was yet another gift of healing where I would unpack the bags I was never meant to carry, one by one. I needed to let go of the weight of the luggage, preventing me from going to new heights. Let me ask you this question. "What are you carrying that is holding you from going higher?" Ponder this as you continue to read.

In this quiet, I found my fight again, rediscovered who I wanted to be, and found my voice. Here, I would pick myself back up again and begin to believe in who I was, and that who I was and could become, would be worth fighting for. I let the divorce finally come off of me. I let the traumas and pains of past wounds go. I told myself that I wasn't allowed to identify as the victim anymore and that I was a victor. I re-told the truths about the battles I had fought. Although they almost took me out, they didn't, and I was still standing. I had to learn when you can do nothing more, simply stand! Get up and get out of your loathing and self-pity. Change your position and posture. From laying down to sitting up to standing, I would learn to walk again. From walking, I would learn to run again. This time, when I would run, I would run without the weight of the bags I had been carrying!

And you will run without the weight of the bags you have been carrying! The forgiveness you chose to walk in. The grace and kindness you decided to give. The strength and courage you claim over fear and worry…This is who you are. The restrictions and limitations have been lifted, and you need to tell yourself the truth that the only one restricting and limiting yourself is you. So again I ask you, "What is it that you are carrying?"

To move forward, you will have to face who you are. And if you don't like who you are and what you see in that mirror, it's time to pivot. Sometimes you have to hate some things in order to change them. Sometimes the only way to get unstuck is to be so deep in mud that there is no question you are neck deep in it, and you can't lie about it anymore. If you settle for untruths and unhealed mindsets, don't be surprised if those unhealed mindsets and truths start going to work with you. What you accommodate will find comfort in the areas of your life, and these uninvited squatters will begin to take up permanent residency and become the uninvited identities you tolerated. Where you go, these mindsets go with you. What you do, these mindsets partner with you. It's time to tell them that you don't need them anymore. It's time to permit yourself to be free and stop tolerating them.

The process of rebuilding who I was, developing my self-worth, and finding my "Why" took about two years to run through and, even now, is not entirely complete. Life is a journey, and the minute we begin to think we have learned all there is to learn, we are shown we have much more to understand. I have finally returned to picking up some new projects, writing, and focusing on my foundation. I am at the point of dreaming again, and the dreams are limitless. Maybe I will help to scale another company. Or perhaps I will write another book after this one is done. Maybe I will create a new company, buy one, continue consulting, or do another development project. I have no idea, but the important thing is that I'm back, and I have promised myself to be a bigger, badder, and healthier version of the "me" than I once was. I am choosing to step out on a new journey and a new phase in my life, free from the baggage I carried before. I am doing it and so can you! Sis, whatever the burden is that you carry through life, let it go. You were never meant to take on the extra weight. Allow yourself the chance to be free from it so you can go higher. You deserve better than what you are giving yourself. Be kind to you and believe you are worth it, because you are! I am writing this book for you. It's taking me a lot of time, and it isn't easy! But I did it for you! I believe in you on the other side of reading this book, and I see you. I care for and am cheering for you!

This new *me* will be able to withstand the storms better, and I won't have to get swallowed by the whale to get to where I am going. I won't need the fake masks I used to wear, and instead of masking my fear with control and pride, I will have the necessary value and confidence to build and create again. And this time, when I do so, I will have the longevity to sustain the process. When I have to fight, I will know what I am fighting for, and if I fall back down again, I will get back up! I will get back up again and again and again because I know what it is I am fighting for. I am fighting for myself and everybody on the other side of me getting back up again! Now re-read this paragraph and read it allowed as though it was you, because this is the new you!

So, get back up again with me, and choose to fight for everything that is waiting for you on the other side: your *vision*, your *purpose*, your *legacy*, your *calling*, and your *message*. People are waiting for you to stand firm again, and when you choose to, the world will be watching, and that light you carry may start as a small light, but it can become the very spotlight that changes the course of the people around you. What is waiting to be birthed from you right now? What is depending on you getting back up and out into the world? What vision can come back to life when you allow yourself to dream again? Choose this moment. The restrictions have been removed, and the limitations uplifted.

Chapter 8

BALANCING THE SEE-SAW

L IFE IS LIKE A SEE-SAW, AND WHEN IT HAS TOO MUCH WEIGHT on one side, no one enjoys the ride... As women, we find ourselves fitting into so many roles. Some of us are wives, mothers, students, caretakers, teachers, employees, entrepreneurs... and the list goes on. We have learned the skill of multi-tasking in juggling through so much of our day-to-day lives. So naturally, we can begin taking on more than we can handle, while trying to find out how to fit into this world.

Social media certainly doesn't help. With Facebook, Instagram, Twitter, and tick-tok, the world has become much smaller, and perceptions of reality have significantly become distorted. These platforms do not help us in finding that balance either. We have created unhealthy comparisons with unrealistic expectations and no legitimized baseline to start from. You only see the good in social media. The bad is left out. You will view what that person wants you to view, and vice versa, see from only fragments of a world you are given access to. You see the "world Traveler." You see the "Influencer." You see the "fashion icon," the "business guru," and the "mom of the year." The personas continue.

I think much of the mental illness that we see in our younger generations stems from the constant comparisons and inability to replicate what is shown in other people's lives… The pursuit of happiness and the lifelong struggle to obtain it. We cannot find balance because what is being shown to us aren't realistic expectations for balancing life. People see that their peers are remarkably thriving, innovating, and re-inventing, and they, by "FOMO," fear they are either inadequate, not doing enough, or simply believe that they are not sufficient. The mountains we end up climbing toward perfection and perceived balance are sky-high and never-ending. These platforms are selling false realities, and we are the ones who are buying and selling. We are both the consumer and the producer. From a marketing and business perspective, it is brilliant! It is, in a sense, a self-sustaining business model. The degradation of family values, rising mental illness within our youth, narcissism, and entitlement mindsets are a growing problem and indirectly re-teaching the next generation how we value each other. We are beginning to value people entirely differently. Get-togethers have become the avenue for the next great photographic setup, and shared memories end up as transactional moments, teaching us just to be surface deep. As a result, we have become a transactional generation.

Instagram will not enable you to find realistic expectations in balancing the lifestyle you decide to pursue. The mom that is a model one day, bakes cakes the next and eats it… builds and runs the empire herself, runs 5 miles daily, and homeschools her kids with frequent zoo and park visits doesn't exist. And if she did, it would come at a great sacrifice to herself and most likely everyone around her, including the empire she is building. Although I believe we can change the world and be incredible moms, great wives, humanitarians, and entrepreneurs, I don't believe that we will find the blueprint on how to get there from social media. That model mom is *werkin* out A LOT, and she probably bought that cake... most definitely didn't eat it, has a team to run that empire, and homeschools her kids with a hired "au pair." What you see is not how they live. That projected balance is a lie. Don't compare how they got there, to how you will get there.

Comparison is the worst tool we can ever use on ourselves because we don't know what others are working with unless they are willing to be transparent and authentic. Transparent with breakdowns, kids crying in the background, and binge-eating, that whole cake isn't sexy enough for social media. Each of us is a unique gift with different strengths, characteristics, and abilities. We each walk a path in life exclusive to ourselves. Revel in that uniqueness and never compare it to others. Never lose sight of the distinct qualities that set you apart. It is what makes you so wonderful. After all, there is only one of you! Don't allow comparison to kill your joy and stifle your creativity.

In addition to not offering realistic expectations for balancing our lives, these social media platforms are teaching us to pursue unhealthy goals. Inarguably, Kym Kardashian is one of our generation's most "Iconic Influencers." Let that sink in.... because that says a lot about where we are as Americans. We don't know her as a humanitarian, an activist, or a woman who changed the world by empowering our youth in remarkable ways like Princess Diana or Mother Teresa had for the Boomer Generation. Instead, we know her as the woman who became famous through her reality television shows and occasionally shows her derriere on tv and magazines. Her reality shows are wrought with strife, family division, over-powering feminism, and the emasculation of the men in their lives. They display superficial materialism, opulent displays of wealth with excessive spending habits, projection of narcissistic mindsets, and the prevalent marketing of "body dysmorphic disorder" to our younger girls. Our generation, unfortunately, grew up in that, and she will forever be responsible for the legacy she is choosing to leave behind.

Now, look at a woman like Amal Clooney, who exudes class and comes from humble beginnings in Beirut, Lebanon. Yet, she chose to make her life purpose-driven, and promulgate a message to change the world and save those without a voice. Amal is the most widely recognized humanitarian lawyer we know, working in the international court systems to tackle crimes against humanity. Her husband is the "Great George Clooney," and he doesn't mind one bit that her career is beginning to outpace his. He casts no shade at his brilliant wife and in fact, parades her around like the magnificent gift she is. He has even taken an interest in securing his family's protection to a greater degree, knowing the risks she takes on to make this world a safer and better place. It comes at a great sacrifice, and they are willing to make it. It can even be suggested that George Clooney has found an even greater purpose through what his wife is doing, and they now embark upon changing the world together.

She is helping to light a spark, and he is helping her to carry that flame. A great man once told me a kite without a string would fly off into the sky. Amal is the kite, and George is the string here, and he is confident enough to own that because he values what she is doing and finds a more significant purpose in what they do together. She gives a voice back to nations that have lost theirs and makes the world a better place! I look up to her in a profound way and she is a hero for our younger girls! This woman has chosen, for whatever reason, not to be on social media. Yet, her legacy is no less remarkable. Rather, it is far more impactful than the women that plague our social media with the trash we continue to buy.

We set the standards for what we are willing to buy. It's time *we*, as a society, raise the bar and say goodbye to the Kyms of this world. We need healthy role models for our generation and can't afford to feed the superficial, the fake, and the unrealistic icons of our generation. Our soul needs to be cleaned and the garbage taken out.

Allowing a cleansing, a reset, and detox from what is toxic, will enable us to look for healthier role models and set more realistic goals for finding balance. We strive for perfection because all others let us see is perfection, and life isn't perfect. Those false expectations we put upon ourselves are exhausting, and will inevitably lead us to burnout. Life is, in fact, like a marathon and not a sprint. We have heard this a million times. But can you imagine if you sprinted the whole marathon as fast as you could? Unless you are a professional runner, you might die before you get there or end up passed out in one of the many medical tents along the way. We can't continue to be consumers of these mindsets, mindsets that don't enable us to find balance and cause us to burn out.

If you are so focused on getting to the finish line, what will you miss along the journey because you forget to just take a break? What will you compromise, lose out on, or not have room for in your sprint to the finish line? How will your family, marriage or relationship, mental and physical health hold up? How will you value the moments along the way, or enjoy the journey, when you are just looking for the next fueling station to get to? And then, what will you do when you get there too early? Finish one race to start another? I have seen great women and men at the top of their game, with nowhere to go, be some of the saddest and loneliest people alive. They have sacrificed their family, their marriages, and for many, their children and have nothing in return to show other than their money.

I was here in 2014, one year into starting a company with two initial partners. Shortly after starting this company, I then branched off to start another company. I was flying every other week to the mainland or going to the outer islands from Oahu, raising two toddlers, and being a wife simultaneously. I was with my ex-husband, with whom I had two children and two more babies with. Let me explain. I had my *own* two physical children, and then I had the companies as the two babies that were both in their infantile states. They needed daily supervision to grow and not fold. My ex-husband was working long hours. We had nannies that helped with the kids, and cleaners were coming on a bi-weekly schedule. I would come home from traveling, or my ex-husband from his traveling, and the dishes wouldn't be done. We would both look at each other and then the dishes. We were exhausted. Things like "who would do the dishes" led to our marriage's demise. I do think it's the small things. Our roles were not clearly defined. He wanted a stay-at-home wife, and I wasn't willing to be that in that season of my life. So, I sacrificed my marriage and my children at the altar of doing business. The businesses survived, but the marriage did not.

I did not balance that season of my life too well and had a lot to learn from it. It was unfortunate that I would have to lose so much for me to learn. As I mentioned at the beginning of the chapter, life is like a see-saw, and when unbalanced, no one enjoys the ride. I would like to say I learned all I needed to in that one season of my life, but I am stubborn, and I did not. It wouldn't be until later that I would fully grasp the importance of balancing life and not rebuilding fallen empires. Empires come, and empires go. Let them go. There is a reason why the fallen ones failed. "A great civilization is not conquered from without until it has destroyed itself from within," stated Ariel Durant. We are creatures of habit. Change is the antithesis of habit, and so unnatural to our mind. Sometimes, you have to let the old mindsets and routines go before you try building new things again, or they will inadvertently turn back into the old things. Running through life so fast, until you run into the ground, is an old mindset that has got to go, so allow it to.

Having daily balance is a good thing. But sometimes, we cannot always find it. For instance, finding balance with your family and loved ones is impossible when starting a new business venture or project. If you start something up that you know will take a lot of your time, try as best as you can to create normalcy for the people who depend on you. Give yourself grace when you cannot. Some things will have to give. Frequently, our health will be the first to go. So, saying no, and knowing your limitations in other areas of your life may be the healthiest thing that can be done for you and your loved ones. If I know I am being stretched in one area, I choose the most important and valuable places to protect and let the others go. Spiritual health, family, and physical health are usually my top priorities. If I have a project going on, I won't spread myself thin with obligations anymore. I will say no to everything other than the priorities I have set forth to finish that project, protect my family, and preserve my health. I now guard my *yes* and do not give it as freely as I once had.

We have to cherish the things we hold near and dear to us while we are building, even if it takes a little more time to do so. If we don't start recognizing the importance of those things and people in our lives, we can hurt or lose them while getting there. Social engagements and goodwill projects are the first to go when I am working on a project. You can always rebuild your social calendar, and helping those in need will be much more meaningful and more manageable when you have the ability to do so. I don't overpromise myself anymore. Our generation has a horrible reputation for overpromising and under-delivering. And when we over-task ourselves and still have to deliver the promise, it can break us down, and then we are over-obligated. I would much rather underpromise and over-deliver.

I also enlist as much help as possible from the outside and focus on my dependent family. I try to keep my spiritual, mental, emotional, and physical health as best as possible. I would have let these areas suffer in the past, but I now understand how vital, healthy well-being is to achieve certain desired outcomes. Dinner may also not be prepared, and if we have to resort to nightly takeout, that is ok. If you have a family, they will remember the time you spent with them, not whether or not you cooked every meal. I try to have more quality moments rather than many not-so-meaningful moments. In addition, "doing life" together is a big thing in our family. My kids have come to meetings with me before. The world is a seemingly more understanding place after Covid; if your situation allows, you may consider including them in your routines. My son and daughter have learned how to adjust and have become less selfish and more independent as a result of my including them in work and life.

Time is the most valuable asset you will ever have, and you can never make up for lost time. Time is the most cherished gift I can ever give someone, and it should also be yours. Treasure and guard your time wisely. By giving it to someone, you are saying that you value and respect them. Think twice about who you give it to. Do they deserve your time, and is it reciprocated? Do they steward or appreciate it as much as you do? If I give you my time, either myself or someone else gets less of it. Time is a gift, and you can tell when others don't appraise it the way that you may. Call me old-fashioned, but I believe that being late is one of the greatest insults you can ever give someone. I grew up being taught that 15 minutes early was on time and on time was late. Aside from mitigating circumstances, when people continuously are tardy, they are inevitably saying that their time is more valuable than yours, which is selfish. And when they give you the "I 'm so sorry, but I'm just really busy," that shouldn't be acceptable if you value yourself at all. Look, the whole world is busy. Whether you are a billionaire or a welfare recipient, time is still time, and you make it for the people that you value in your life, and if you can't do so respectfully, don't over-commit in the first place. Re-access what and who you give your time to and whether or not these areas and people deserve your time. I am sure you will find that there are opportunities for you to improve upon as well.

Even a balanced see-saw goes up and goes down. If ridden, it never stays perfectly balanced. Such is the same with life. When one area in your life receives all the attention, and time allows, begin to switch your focus on the other areas that were neglected. While working on my development project for several years, I took a break to focus on rebuilding my health and family over the next couple of years. It took that long to rebuild because things had gotten so severely off balance. I am not advocating for you to go for years, neglecting one area of your life. That is a recipe for disaster, and that path leads toward burnout. As a result of my pitfalls, I have found a much more balanced approach. The length in between has gotten shorter and has become more meshed or blended together. However, I am stating that if you find yourself having neglected something important, go back to it and strengthen it. We can't expect to have a perfect balance all the time. Just the soonest that you notice and can, try to rebalance that portion of your life. Hopefully, this balancing act will get better and easier as time goes on.

Balance with work is difficult to maintain, but the same goes for raising children. I remember going through my divorce and fighting for the custody of my kids. As I mentioned in earlier chapters, it was a very difficult time for me to go through. I was not in a healthy state of being during or after this period. I practically won full custody, which was a major win. I only had to share my children in the summer and during two rotating holidays a year. When that battle was won, I was fighting two other almost simultaneous legal battles, and so I was exhausted and in survival mode. I got my kids, and I held on to them. I only shared, by law, what was court-ordered and not a day more.

When you fight so hard for something, you know its value and aren't willing to let it go so easily. However, as time progressed and healing set in, I was able to do what was right for the children, and so now, the kids get as much of their biological dad as they need or want. As a result, we have an extremely healthy co-parenting style that benefits the children immensely, and both my ex-husband and current husband get along exceptionally well. I absolutely adore my ex-husband's wife and I really couldn't have asked for a better mom to step into my place when I am not there. We are seen as the modern-day extended family and have worked really hard to get to where we are today. It works. The kids are happy. The parents are happy, and we have a pretty healthy co-parenting style.

Looking back, I held onto my kids in an unhealthy way. Even holding too tightly to your children can not only hold you back but can also hold them back from progressing and growing. Now, when the kids are gone, I don't cry for the whole summer and stop living as I once had. Instead, I rest, focus on strengthening my marriage and entrepreneurial projects, travel a bit, and catch up with my friends. I allow this time to give myself a reset so that when they return to me, I am able to focus on their needs.

Balance is a complicated thing to maintain, and anyone that claims that they have truly mastered it... Well, perhaps some skepticism would be well-suited. It is an ongoing project that is constantly having us pivot, readjust and realign our lives. We are up in one area one day and down the next, riding on the see-saw that is life. While riding it, set realistic expectations, give healthy boundaries, guard your *yes,* and remember to give yourself some grace.

Chapter 9

BOUNDARIES

A RE YOU GETTING UP YET! WE'VE DISCUSSED SO MANY important concepts, such as dreaming again and finding your purpose and your "Roar!" We discussed legacy, balance, and overcoming obstacles. Now, this may be the most important yet shortest chapter that I am writing in this book. It is also, for some, the most painful lesson to learn in our personal lives and in business. But it's also reasonably straightforward, so I won't spend too much time on it. This chapter is on boundaries and why having them will save you from wasting time, money, stress, therapy... you fill in the blank.

Boundaries and exercising the use of them are vital to your emotional well-being and even physical health. They will protect you from unscrupulous business partners and deals and even provide a guide on how to exercise caution under challenging circumstances. I have often found that a lack of boundaries was the primary reason for a lot of misplaced anger. I was angry because I found myself being taken advantage of. I was even more furious at myself for allowing me to get there in the first place. Boundaries are the limit within which you are willing to entertain an action, a thought, or a circumstance in your life. The Merriam Webster Dictionary defines boundaries as "something that indicates or fixes a limit or extent." It is, in essence, *the line of demarcation.* Or, as Merriam-Webster also defines it, "the marking of the limits or boundaries of something."

Do you have healthy boundaries in your business life? Can you say no to the things that don't serve you, your values, your goals, and your vision? Are you able to take a break from toxic people in your life and even say no to a deal that you know will inevitably overextend your limits? Boundaries are very simple to create. If you know what you are willing and unwilling to do… you can start there. You have to assess your personal boundaries, which will be created largely by your values and limits. Let me ask you this. In previous chapters, we worked on personal values, identity, and confidence. Are you able to now value yourself more and put those boundaries into practice? This is the next step in moving forward with constructing a healthy workflow. Setting up structures and routines around you will allow you to thrive better and serve as limits to those you do business with. Having strict professional relationships will generate respect from your colleagues. Understanding and respecting others' boundaries will likewise often elicit a reciprocal response as well.

Saying yes to everyone and everything does not make you *Superwoman.* It makes you overwhelmed, spread thin, and unable to deliver prime results with the same precision as if it were prioritized to a greater degree. Saying yes to everyone also devalues your help. It's seen as… expected, is often taken advantage of, and will be taken for granted. When you say "yes," as we learned in the earlier chapter, what are you saying no to? Your family? Your *own* priorities? Are you having to now run from one commitment, only to be late and unprofessional to the next? You should guard your "yes" and use your "no" more often. People will respect you more for it. They will know when you say yes to something, you mean it and value what they are asking because you believe it's important enough to set aside your time to see it through.

The entrepreneurial space has a lot of different types of personalities you have to deal with. If you don't have boundaries, you may even find yourself in a co-dependent space, discovering that you are now in an emotionally exhausting and abusive situation, allowing toxic relationships to thrive. And don't blame them. Blame yourself. You got yourself into it, not the other way around. You are the *only* one responsible for your allowance of what you are willing to tolerate. Let me repeat that... YOU are the *ONLY* one responsible. I know this sounds harsh, but you need to hear it and take ownership of your outcomes. I am sure that even as you are reading this, many of you may be relating to your own circumstances or situations because we have all experienced this at one point or another. You may have even been the ones dishing it out at times. That's ok. This is a great time to re-assess and re-adjust so that you can create a healthy working dynamic for yourself *and* the people around you.

And by the way, boundaries aren't just for you to exercise on everyone else. Sometimes, you need to be the one practicing boundaries on your *own* self. Sometimes you need to place some tape on that mouth of yours and stop it from self-destructing you! Trumpeting everything you do to everyone around you has never been the wisest strategy in business. Business is competitive. Remember that. People say, "*business is business*" for a reason. What that means is, at the end of the day, the only thing that matters is business, and to some people, it supersedes everything in between. So, sharing your business proposal with everyone out there, just so they can see how smart you are and maybe or maybe not invest in it, will not work to your advantage. Keep those things private and locked up tight. Use your discernment. Practice some wisdom and discretion. Business is nasty. Wherever there is business, there is money. Wherever there is money, there is greed. As the saying goes, greed corrupts good company.

So, if you do have a great business idea that has the potential to make a lot of money, that idea also has the potential to be stolen and copied. Remember earlier, in Chapter 7, on *Growing in the Dark*, we spoke about your dream being like a seed planted underground. Your dream is that seed "growing in the dark," and that if it comes up too early, without the proper rooting system and time needed to mature to withstand the elements, it could die. This is where that allegory meets your business. So, if you have an incredible dream or vision, keep it to yourself until you know that you are in front of the right people to share it with and that the timing is perfect.

Not all of those within your sphere of influence will be your cheerleaders. Not all of those that are within your inner circle are people that you can trust. People wear masks to disguise their hidden motives all the time. People can be haters. You may place your trust in the wrong person, only to receive the "kiss of Judah" next, and some people get immoral when it comes to making money. Don't automatically assume the person you are talking with has your best intentions, even if they are your friend. People are people and only humans. We are flawed, get jealous, and make bad decisions. I have seen even the best of friends play on another's trust in business. I have even seen my own lack of judgment in character come to knife me in the back. When you are a child, it is cute to be unassuming and naive. When you are a grown female entrepreneur, it is dangerous to operate with such naivete. And I'm sorry to be dishing it out to you with such a tone, but somehow you got pulled down, and we need to make sure it doesn't happen again. We need to ensure you aren't going to be making the same mistakes as we go forward.

Well, this book is about getting up, overcoming obstacles, and bouncing back after one too many rounds in the "boxing ring." You are most likely reading this as a reactionary result of not exercising the proper boundaries that knocked you out in the first place. In the future, prevention will be correlative to boundary creation. It will save you a lot of headaches and heartbreak in the long run, and placing those boundaries in your workspace may help you from getting knocked down in the first place.

Chapter 10

THE PIONEER

E LIZABETH BLACKWELL ONCE STATED, "IT IS NOT EASY TO BE A
pioneer- but oh, it is fascinating! I would not trade one
moment, even the worst moment, for all the riches in the world."
Elizabeth went on to become Dr. Elizabeth, the first female
doctor in the United States, even opening a medical college for
women. Elizabeth Blackwell is a *pioneer* who paved the way for
women to become doctors in the United States. Because of her
pioneering, countless women have reaped the benefits of her
persistent determination. Pioneering is the most arduous road to
travel. In fact, I believe it is the most ambitious thing to do in
business. If you are pioneering, you will often find yourself alone,
on the edge of discovering something new, and trying to break
through to bring forth what has never been done before. You
are the *establishment changer,* the *trendsetter,* the *revolutionist,* the
innovator, and the *pathfinder.* You have a vision that the rest of
the world may not be quite ready for. That is why you are "The
Pioneer!"

Early American pioneers had no path. They had to create it in the wilderness. Just like the early American Pioneers, you will find yourself alone in a wilderness, with no clear path forward, and often up against a status quo that will not be easy to change. You may find that the wilderness may seem to be a barren place. You may find yourself wanting to give up, turn around and throw in the towel. You may even find yourself giving up on "THE DREAM" in the process. But pioneering is about exploring, making your mark, and planting your flag. It's about answering the innate call back to the wilderness to explore the great unknown, and if you give up on your dream too early, you may never find what you were meant to discover!

In 1804, an expedition to the "West" began. Lewis and Clark mapped out the newly purchased frontier, named the "Louisiana Purchase," bought from Napoleon's France the year prior. By doing so, President Thomas Jefferson was able to acquire the land he wanted to expand into America, while, at the same time, relieving France of its debt obligations from a series of expensive wars. In the process of pioneering this newly acquired land, Lewis and Clark's expedition suffered many privations. To begin with, they had insufficient support and resources for what they set out to do.

Even knowing of the difficulties they would face, Lewis and Clark chose to answer the call and led the expedition into the great unknown. They paved the way for an "early settlement" to follow in expanding America westward and are now a part of American History. They discovered new plant life, created treaties with Native American tribes, and mapped out the purchased territories for the United States Government. It came at a significant cost and sacrifice, but they believed it was worth pursuing. The road was long and arduous and certainly untraveled. What road are you looking at that is perhaps the road less traveled? What path are you pioneering or want to pioneer that may change your future and potentially impact the world? In the early 1900's Robert Frost once wrote a poem titled "The Road Not Taken."

The Road Not Taken
By Robert Frost

Two roads diverged in a yellow wood,
And sorry I could not travel both
And be one traveler, long I stood
And looked down one as far as I could
To where it bent in the undergrowth;

Then took the other, as just as fair,
And having perhaps the better claim,
Because it was grassy and wanted wear;
Though as for that the passing there
Had worn them really about the same,

And both that morning equally lay
In leaves no step had trodden black.
Oh, I kept the first for another day!
Yet knowing how way leads on to way,
I doubted if I should ever come back.

I shall be telling this with a sigh
Somewhere ages and ages hence:
Two roads diverged in a wood, and I—
I took the one less traveled by,
And that has made all the difference.

This poem is about individuality and perseverance. It's about looking at a difficult decision and choosing the unknown over complacency. It's about forging our paths in life, accepting the risks, finding hope, and believing there is a reward waiting for us on the other side. We can relate this to real-life thinking and patterns in business. We can't take every path. We can't choose the road less traveled and choose the road more convenient. They are usually mutually exclusive. As Robert Frost states in the end, "Two roads diverged in a wood, and I— I took the one less traveled by, And that has made all the difference." He chose the road less traveled, and it changed his life. Robert Frost wrote as a pioneer, and he held the pen. When you *pioneer*, you wield the pen and write the future. What will your future look like? What will you write or re-write that may very well have the ability to transform your future and your legacy? What uncharted territory will you discover as you choose the paths less taken?

We need strong, confident women willing to take on the less traveled roads, become pioneers, and stand out against the crowd. It takes courage to embark upon a journey that you may not know the outcome of, but individualism and courage are needed in today's business climate more than ever. Unfortunately, we are evolving into a society where courage has declined, and we find our younger generations more apathetic and less passionate. We are failing them when we go before them and choose the path of apathy and passivity. You have to have passion so that you can create and celebrate individual achievements with those pioneering forward.

We have created a culture that looks to favor assimilation over individual expression. Fear has captivated our culture. Our youth are watching us and looking for role models. The *Millennials* are looking for mentors, and the *Boomers* are getting ready to transition into retirement, waiting for the next generations to reach their purpose. Strong and confident leaders will be needed to bridge the gap as the generations begin to transition. The world is watching, and we are all looking for those who will stand out in the face of formidable opposition and choose to overcome through the road less traveled. Pioneers will be needed to pave new paths forward, and fear has no place in the wilderness.

We live in a society where hope is barely floating above the water and can be sunk to the bottom of the sea at any given moment, buried like treasure needing to be re-discovered. Fear is contagious, but so too is hope! The pen you hold will be able to write this message of hope, but courage will be needed to wield your pen and chart the future that is before you.

Elon Musk is perhaps one of the most valuable pioneers in the history of American Technology. He once said, "If something is important enough, even if the odds are stacked against you, you should still do it." And you should still do it… even if the odds are stacked terribly against you! I have often found that sheer determination and persistence will eventually push those doors open, and if it is that important to you, you will have the passion needed to follow it. Elon didn't stop when he created the meritorious technological revolution in driving, Tesla. He started by creating cars powered solely by electricity. He continues to challenge himself with new ventures, including SpaceX, Open AI, Neuralink, and even Twitter. He is an innovator and challenges companies to do better and to be better while advancing several entirely different industries, from cars to rockets to AI technology.

Founding Tesla, Elon Musk challenged the entire global car manufacturing industry worth trillions of dollars to do better and be better in reducing both their carbon emissions and lowering their carbon footprint overall. Elon Musk stated, "When I was in college, I wanted to be involved in things that would change the world." And he did change the world. It is a better place because of the technology he gave to the world. He pioneered the electric car and continues to pioneer in every sector he influences, and because of his contributions to society, we live in a better world.

Another great technological innovator of our time was the late Steve Jobs, who started the trillion-dollar computer company Apple in his garage. Steve was also a pioneer in how he thought and revolutionized the world. There isn't a person in America, or in the developed world for that matter, that hasn't been influenced by the impact of his company or owns one of the products he developed, including your iPhone.

To stand out, you will not be able to fit in, and pioneers never worry about fitting in. They are too busy innovating! They are looking to stand out from the crowd. The late Steve Jobs once stated one of my favorite quotes,

"Here's to the crazy ones.
The misfits.
The rebels, the troublemakers,
The round pegs in the square holes...
The ones who see things differently-
They're not fond of rules...
You can quote them, disagree with them,
glorify or vilify them
But the one thing you can't do is ignore them
Because they change things.
Because the ones who are crazy enough
to think they can change the world, are the ones who do.
Think Different."

I live by this quote. I have rarely found myself fitting in. The world is far too big and magnificent to allow myself to be constrained and restricted by it. You must be willing to stand out from the crowd to find yourself leading the crowd, doing great things. You will have to be willing to go against what others think and even be willing to be booed by them at times. Sometimes, the only one you will find cheering you on and in your corner is you, and that may have to be enough. To be different and to do great things will be to travel that road less traveled, and others may not always be able to come with you. Often, people can simply see your vision. However, being an innovator usually means having a greater vision than those around you. Their resistance may stem from an inability to see what you see. Sometimes it's not even that they don't want to come with you or want to reject your vision.

Sometimes people can't understand the novelty associated with your vision, and aren't willing to risk what you are willing to risk for it.

Because being different is to be a pioneer, and when you are a pioneer, you will be on a frontier that has not yet been traversed. There will be no paved road or even a map of how to get there. There will be no rules. You will have to set the standard. You are "pioneering," and so those that want to change the world will often be the ones that get to make the new world!

Chapter 11

THE CHEERLEADER

H AVE YOU EVER HEARD THE SAYING, "YOU CAN'T HOLD A TORCH to light another's path without brightening yours? It's so true. Helping others will always create brightness and bring light to the things you do. How can you light another's path without your own being lit up in the process… literally speaking? It's an allegory to what happens to us as we lift other people up. Booker T Washington stated, "If you want to lift yourself up, lift someone else up."

As you run your race, let me ask you something… are you a cheerleader? I don't mean literally, with pom poms and all… but do you cheer those around you? Are you happy for your peers when they succeed? Can you cheer their success even when you find yourself in stagnation? These are essential questions to ask yourself while reading this chapter.

When I was younger, as previously shared, I was a tomboy. I rode bikes, jumped off dirt mounds I helped to build, snowboarded in the winters, and surfed in the summers. Even as I got older, I continued hanging out with the boys, rock climbing, riding dirt bikes, and finding new adventures. I still do to this day. Nothing much has changed. Only when I got into college and started making more friends that were girls, I realized girls were very different than boys, had a little more drama, and were a bit more emotional. This was a learning curve for me. I like to say I was raised to be a boy.... Not to any fault of my mother, she really tried to instill the more "gentile" qualities in me, which I do believe came out a little later in life. Still, she is a very strong, 1st Generation American Woman, originally from South Korea, and was simply outnumbered by the men in my family.

I love my mother, and she raised me to be strong. There is something beautiful about 1st Generation American Women. If you know one, you know what I mean. They were just cut from a different cloth. They know how to persevere, are supernaturally strong, and can overcome almost anything. They know how to survive and don't back down in the face of fear. I love my mother's strength. It is a different kind of strength, the kind of *strong* that has seen war tear apart her country and rebuild her home amidst the challenges that came from it. The kind of *strong* that sacrificed her education to help feed her family of 6. The kind of strong that grew up without a father and became the missing role model for an entire family. She knew what it meant to persevere, to not have, and to overcome every possible limitation to make her way to America and receive a better life for her children. I am proud to call her my mother and am blessed to be raised under the strength of who she is.

My Sister-in-Law is also cut from this same cloth. Her strength is encouraging, and her persistence is admirable. She keeps me on my toes with gratitude. She would always say, "What is there to complain about? We are happy, have shelter and food, and we have all we want or need. There is no room ever to complain." She certainly doesn't complain and is also another 1st Generation American Woman from her home country, Peru. We need these types of women that come to America and help to remind us to be strong because we are better together! This is the history and present-day culture that makes America so great and gives us our fortitude! I am also proud to call her my Sister-In-Law. Just like my mother, she helps me to be a better woman, because as mentioned, we are better together! We are stronger together. There is a place where women can all go forward together, and that is toward a healthy future!

I have often apologized for being a strong woman in my youth. Now, I repel the very idea of apologizing for being strong and subordinating the opinion of women for the sake of their husbands and the men around them. Having been raised by a strong woman, I don't think there is anything wrong with that in today's world. I believe if you think there is, it may have been because you had a bad experience with an overpowering woman in a negative way, and that has negatively shaped how you view those women, and I am so sorry for that. For men who think strong women need to soften, I also think this may be more of an opportunity for those men to step up and be more assertive, and that issue will become obsolete. If we have stronger men in our society, they won't be bothered by stronger women. We then strengthen how we go forward, and not weaken who we are to go backward.

As I stated in Chapter 2, I was raised to be a lady. I shared how my mother tried very hard to teach me how to have those qualities. I do not believe the qualities of being a strong independent woman in any way negate you from having the qualities of femininity which I celebrate. Confident mature men celebrate strong women and have no problem standing behind their women at times. My husband epitomizes this statement. As the sturdy man he is, he is confident enough to let me be all the woman I am and want to be. As a mature woman, I also take the time to build my man up and encourage him to be the competent and mentally indestructible man he is. I don't want to shine at my husband's expense and vice versa. We want to lift each other up in the process of whatever we are pursuing together. Is it perfect? Absolutely not, but every day we work at it, and every day we put in the time needed so we can handle what our present-day circumstances or future may require from us.

We work hard to have a healthy marriage in a modern-day world that doesn't support the institution of it, and it's a daily thing. It's also not easy and will require your dedication and time commitment. However, as you continue to expand and grow in your successes, your marriage will need the investment, so you don't have to lose it in the process, as I did. And, if you're not married, that is ok too! Just skip over this part, and take notes for your future, or don't! Just like having children, it's not for everyone and is a profoundly personal decision. It makes you no less of an incredible and successful woman for choosing not to either. It's ok not to be married or want to be. I shared in earlier chapters about Mother Theresa not being married or having children and yet finding great purpose along her journey. We are far too often told that marriage and children are the only way to find true happiness and that doing so, will solve all of our problems. I would strongly disagree with this notion. It's esoteric and not correlative to finding purpose.

However, in the event that you are married or want to be, building each other up is an investment you will want to make. My husband and I try not to provide room for insecurity. We spend time reassuring and reaffirming each other because confidence takes work and application to co-exist in a marriage. Insecure men often feel threatened by strong women because they can't control them. Women were never meant to be controlled. That is a dysfunction in it and of itself. I have seen men wield power over women with finances, security, and even love. It's an abhorrent and degrading practice. Women need to be able to express themselves freely and be who they were created to be. They also need to feel loved and desired.

A confident man provides the security and stability for a woman to really soar, and when you see a woman on top, a woman who has really made it, if we can admit it, there may be a great man behind her, cheering her forward. And ladies, they do exist! I promise. You might have just not found the right one yet! So, like the saying goes for men, "Behind every great man, there is a great woman." Well, I would like to also infer that, "Behind every great woman, there *may* be a great man!" Now, please don't misquote what I am saying here as the absolute reference for great women, as there will obviously be many exceptions to this. My point is, it is ok to build up men in our society and give credit when due as we, women, also come up! We don't have to feel the need to prove to the world that we don't need men and we did it all on our own. That notion is toxic and may come from an unhealed mindset with the opposite sex that may have hurt you. I am also deeply sorry for this, but understand that we can become stronger and healed together if we are willing to move forward. And if we are able to let go of some of these pains, we can go much further in the process.

In the movie, "Barbie©," Ryan Gosling plays Ken and Margot Robbie plays Barbie. In a GQ video he is promoting the movie in, Ryan Gosling states

"Just remember that behind every great Barbie, there's a Ken, who's totally fine with that. Hopefully he's right behind her, in case she needs anything. Because she deserves it. Because she's Barbie and he's just Ken. And he's totally fine with that... forever"

This is a timely monologue reflecting the need for the world to shift and make room for what a successful woman can look like with a supportive man by her side. In the monologue, Ken is stating this. I believe as successful women, we can likewise be confident enough to express this ourselves towards the men that help to hold us up and give them the credit they deserve when they earn it.

Great women are also not afraid to push back, be independent, and even be somewhat rebellious! In the famous movie, "My Fair Lady," the late and great Audrey Hepburn plays a beautiful young flower girl that an English Professor takes in, as a bet he could make a young *lady* out of a practically homeless girl with horrible grammar and manners. Liza Doolittle is made fit to be a princess and dances and intrigues the heart of a handsome young prince by the end of the film. Professor Higgin's celebrated when Liza rebelled throughout her lessons, calling her a *consort battleship*. Healthy femininity and independent strength should be admired as desired characteristics for all women. They are not antithetical qualities. I believe you can have both. I was raised with the boys to be highly independent, but as I grew older and became a woman, I began championing my inner feminity!

My father is also a very masculine man, but not in a nasty misogynistic way... he is actually a very compassionate and caring human being. After a long dedication to serving our country in the military, he became a nurse anesthetist and historical author. He always told me that war was not what you see in the movies and never really wanted to discuss it too much. He told me that he went into nursing because, after fighting for our country, he wanted to now serve those who were sick and in need of help. He even spends his time going into the prison systems with baked cookies to spread love and kindness to the inmates. And on Saturdays, like clockwork, he hands out water and food to the people experiencing homelessness that live in his community.

Well, as I mentioned earlier, I was still raised by an Army Ranger, and in addition to all of that, I also had two brothers that loved to treat me like another brother. So, on the weekends growing up, my dad would take us all to the park, and we would play football together, and I grew up throwing that football like a guy. I was best friends with my brothers and love them dearly. To this day, we talk regularly. In Highschool, I spent most of my time hanging around my older brother. I always felt like we were more like twins, and had it not been for him, High School would have been rough.

So, I grew up in a household where family was extremely important. My older brother was raised to take care of and look after me and my younger brother. All this to say, femininity was more of a learned afterthought and became more interwoven into who I was as I got a little older. I was much more accustomed to hanging around guys growing up. So, the differences became a bit more stark when I began making more girlfriends.

When I was 18, I went off to college in Hawaii and took on several jobs to pay for it. In addition, I was writing for the school newspaper and interning at a news station in downtown Honolulu. At that point in my life, I wanted to become a Broadcast Journalist and save the world, like we all do when we are young and aspiring. So, life was hectic, and I was highly exposed to the world of girls and drama. I mainly worked with women and found it to be incredibly onerous to navigate at times. Needless to say, there was a lot of jealousy, backstabbing, and gossip that I was not entirely prepared to endure. In my personal life, I still hung out with the boys. That is where I felt most safe and comfortable.

It wasn't really until I went through some major life changes in my later 20s that I started finding the right type of *girl team*, where I could also become a cheerleader of other women. To this day, some of my best and longest friendships were with guys I met in college. However, the transition allowed me to expand my *girl tribe* and find my people… During this shift, and somewhere in between, I started making more intelligent choices about the women with whom I became friends. I started making friends with women who were confident, strong, independent, and could carry their own weight as I could. You have to level up your circle when you level up, or you might find yourself being brought down and unchallenged. As I pursued these healthier friendships, the former issues began to dissolve.

Haven't you ever heard the saying, "You are who you hang around with?" Well, it's true, and if it's garbage, and they stink, you stink too. So, don't let yourself stink. Hang around people you want to be like, that actually like you. You shouldn't be the smartest or most successful one in the bunch, and you don't need to feed your ego. You need to feed your drive! And if someone doesn't want to play nice with you anymore and is childish enough to cut you out of their life, thank them for doing you a favor. Burning relationships can be a sign of a personality disorder you do not want to entertain in your life, and that goes for you too… Try not to burn any bridges. Being able to exit gracefully says a lot about who you are. Boundaries and leveling up your social circle are different from burning bridges. You can still cross over if you need to later. However, if someone burns that bridge with you… As Queen Elsa in Frozen says, Let it go….. QUEEN, Let them go….. Pruning is a necessary process, so allow it! It allows room for what can grow next. Although it can hurt, please don't allow the rejection to hurt you, it can sometimes be the best thing for you.

I realized that confident and independent women were less likely to be caught up in gossip and jealousy. How many of us know that if your friend is sharing gossip with you, then they are 100% sharing gossip on you? If you doubt this, it is a problem of understanding at the most basic of human behavioral levels, and you may need to explore a deeper understanding of this. It's a character and integrity issue. Also, if your friends are coming to you with gossip, that means they know you are willing to entertain it, and you do not want that reputation.

Certain types of people gossip. It was most likely interwoven into their character at an early age. If this is you, it's ok, just pivot. People gossip because it makes them feel better about themselves. The face value of this reality may be painful. If you find yourself gossiping, ask yourself why it is that sharing something negative that is going on in your friend's life makes you feel better. The same goes for judging and criticizing. Why does it make you feel better? It's not them. It's you. It's your internal dialogue that needs healing. So allow yourself that healing. We have all engaged with it at one point or another. Just do better, and don't do it going forward. We need strong and confident women in today's society. However, of more importance, we need strong, confident, and *whole* women more than ever as our future business leaders!

So, these new friendships I had made were women who were confident in themselves, which was the key. We are raised in an era where competitiveness and comparison are at the core of our value system, and we often compare and compete with the very people we should be cheering and lifting up. We are raised to think that winning and being the best takes priority over human value, and we do anything to feed our egos, even if it means slandering someone because you're allowing yourself to be a sore loser and jealous that you didn't do better.

Whatever happened to team building, cheering, and bringing each other up so we can win together? Now, I don't believe in community participation medals, and I think they are the worst things in assessing achievement and evaluating worth and only further "entitlement issues." I do believe there is value in 1st place. But whatever happened to shaking the victor's hand after the soccer game you lost in elementary school? What happened to being competitive because you know you can do better, and you are challenging yourself to be the best version of who you can be? Compete against yourself and not everyone in the room. There is a difference. To win against everyone in the room and have that be your sole desire will leave you an empty room with no one to share your medal with. To be a winner, you have to share wins, cheer others' victories, and bring up the ones around you that lose.

I was listening to this business podcast the other day, and it was talking about how this guy asked a very successful billionaire what the keys to success were in raising capital for his funds. He told him that one of the secrets was in the way in which he networked. He said that you have to get your information out in such a way that doesn't make you sound arrogant or like you're reading your resume. He went on to say that he worked with a partner that would be his pitch guy and cheerleader and vice versa. They would work a room together, and each would be talking the other up until every person in that room would eventually meet the "other partner." People would know how successful their past projects were before they even met them. When they did meet the "other guy," they would already have a very positive view associated with them because their reputation preceded them. This shows you how powerful a tool it can be to have someone cheering for you, for someone to be in your corner.

A lot of people don't like to share. However, sharing shows that you are confident and secure enough to do so. It shows that your source won't run out, even if you spend the time giving to others. Lifting up other people helps you to exude that confidence. It radiates and can easily be recognized. Conversely, if you win by destroying everyone but you, your reputation will spread fast! At your slightest mistakes, the knives will come out, and the sharks will circle.

We have to do better in lifting up other women. That fake over-powering feminist movement won't work out either. Just like misogyny was out with the 90s, so is that nasty emasculating movement. It may have found purpose in prior decades, but it's now time to re-fresh, re-brand, and modernize how we choose to be viewed and celebrate each other! Start your own girls' club and be the biggest cheerleader out there! People love a cheerleader. Look at social media. People are begging to be recognized and would love to know that someone is in their corner. Whenever you see your friends, build them up. Tell them how beautiful they look, notice their achievements, and join in cheering their successes as though they were yours and SISTER…don't forget to smile. It will make you feel and look better!

Speaking of sisterhood, I don't feel like I could possibly write this book without including Gloria's monologue in Greta

Gerwig's Barbie©. Gloria is an employee for Matel and goes on a journey in the pursuit of reigniting purpose and passion. Gloria delivered a monologue about unrealistic expectations put upon women. In it, she states,

"It is literally impossible to be a woman. You are so beautiful, and so smart, and it kills me that you don't think you're good enough. Like, we have to always be extraordinary, but somehow we're always doing it wrong.

"You have to be thin, but not too thin. And you can never say you want to be thin. You have to say you want to be healthy, but also you have to be thin. You have to have money, but you can't ask for money because that's crass. You have to be a boss, but you can't be mean. You have to lead, but you can't squash other people's ideas. You're supposed to love being a mother, but don't talk about your kids all the damn time. You have to be a career woman but also always be looking out for other people. You have to answer for men's bad behaviour, which is insane, but if you point that out, you're accused of complaining. You're supposed to stay pretty for men, but not so pretty that you tempt them too much or that you threaten other women because you're supposed to be a part of the sisterhood.

"But always stand out and always be grateful. But never forget that the system is rigged. So find a way to acknowledge that but also always be grateful. You have to never get old, never be rude, never show off, never be selfish, never fall down, never fail, never show fear, never get out of line. It's too hard! It's too

contradictory and nobody gives you a medal or says thank you! And it turns out in fact that not only are you doing everything wrong, but also everything is your fault.

"I'm just so tired of watching myself and every single other woman tie herself into knots so that people will like us. And if all of that is also true for a doll just representing women, then I don't even know."

And it literally can be impossible to be a woman! Whether you know it or not, that girl next to you is wrestling with the same thoughts that you are. She is going through the same difficulties you are going through and is wrestling with self-worth, identity, balance, value and expectations that the world, and we as women, put upon our selves just like Gloria did! So be gracious to you and to the women you meet!

Spend your time building up the women around you. They will, in return, want to do the same for you! Cheerlead their latest accomplishments. You don't know what the woman across from you may be dealing with and don't only care about what is important to you! The world is looking for connection and what is real. People can see through fake and self-serving. Even in your valley, you will be much happier when you help someone else reach their mountain! Narcissism is being exposed in our generation in an ugly way, and you don't want to be the last one to realize that it's… ugly!

So, go and get some Botox, attack those 11s, and stop looking so angry in all your pictures! Start smiling, be happy, and be the biggest cheerleader out there! Yes, you can be successful and not look like you have something to prove while setting a poor example for the rest of our gender. If you become an innovator, by default, you will become a leader. Be a good one! All good leaders lead by example. No good leader asks others to do, what they are not willing to do. Lead by example and be the woman you want your daughter to grow up to be, and become the kind of woman you want your son to marry. They watch how you lead and will become or marry whatever you reflect. So, reflect the best version of you! Lift other women up when you come up, and you will find your tribe!

Chapter 12

BUILDING WINGS

T HERE IS A SAYING THAT IF YOU ARE BORN POOR, IT IS NOT your fault, but if you die poor, it is, and I would agree with this statement. For the most part, if you are born in the USA, no matter your station in life or where you come from, there really isn't much you can't do if you put your mind to it!

The author and writer of the Harry Potter series, J. K Rowlings, was just about as poor as you could be without being homeless. She was on welfare, and government housing assistance without a job, raising her child, and now she's a billionaire. BOOM! I know very successful people who have had backstories of sex, drugs, rock and roll, and homelessness that went on to create multi-million dollar organizations. What's your excuse? There ultimately is none. What set these people apart and made their stories different? I think they were thirsty. They had a hunger, maybe literally…that fueled the fire in them!

I also understand that we aren't all born with a silver spoon in our mouth. However, some of the most successful people have come from nothing, and they wanted it badder than anyone else in that room did. So, they got the success they were hungry for. I do also empathize that it's not like we grow up wanting to die with our dreams in our graves. That often times, life knocks you down, making it so difficult to get back up. That is why I wrote this book! I understand that there are obstacles along the way, with people pushing you down and life just getting in the way… but this book is about pushing through no matter how difficult it has been and no matter the cards you have been dealt! It's about getting up and not settling for victimization and excuses, and it's time to reach deep and *get up*! Girl, it's time to get UP!

It's time to get your grind on! It's time to start firing back up those dusty engines and get your drive back! Let's put things into perspective for a moment and get real… However old you are now, is a lot younger than you will be in the future. You are gettin' older every day, and that's a fact. So, girl, what are you going to do? Spend the prime of your life getting over your sad story? Focusing on everything that's been done to you… you can't do this, can't do that, been through this, been through that? Come on, are you gonna get your grind on when your 80, with your shaky old knees and a wheelchair to carry you? You are in your prime now! So, get off of that couch! Get out and in front of that excuse, and stop playing to the tune of surrender! There is nothing that you can't do if you are willing to put away your pride, humble yourself, and get back up again. Stop looking around at who's watching you, who's been closing those doors and talking trash. Be a good example, be somebody's hero, BE STRONG and Get up GIRL!

I wrote earlier about your purpose and your "why." If you have a dream big enough, and a purpose to carry you through, sheer persistence will get you through to the other side. *Purpose* is on the other side of you getting back up, and persistence and determination will get you there.

Lady Gaga is an excellent example of this. She may be one of the most creative female musicians of all time, and it certainly didn't come easy to her. It started at age four with classical piano lessons followed by open mic trials, ongoing auditions, and musical and theatrical schooling. She faced a lot of rejection and closed doors, but Lady Gaga had a persistent determination to get back up over and over again. If she allowed the rejection, the opinion of her peers, and the surrounding circumstances to determine her outcome, she wouldn't be where she is today. To date, she has won thirteen Grammy Awards, an Academy Award, two Golden Globe Awards, and many other awards, including breaking several Guinness World Records. And in 2019, Lady Gaga stole our hearts in the movie, "A Star Is Born," and even went on to win an Oscar for the "Best Original Song Academy Award" for *Shallow*. She gave a beautiful acceptance speech stating,

> *"Thank you for believing in us. Thank you so much. And if you are at home, and you're sitting on your couch, and you're watching this right now, all I have to say is that this is hard work. I've worked hard for a long time, and it's not about, you know...it's not about winning. But what it's about is not giving up. If you have a dream, fight for it. There's a discipline for*

passion. And it's not about how many times you get rejected or you fall down or you're beaten up. It's about how many times you stand up and are brave and you keep on going. Thank you!"

It *is* about not giving up! It is about fighting for your dream, and getting back up, no matter how many times you fall! Don't allow the low moments in time to define your outcome. Don't allow the last project to be your best project. Your former days to be your "glory" days. Don't set out to pasture before the most beautiful chapters of your life are written! There is a future waiting for you, and the best is yet to come! Remember that your words have power, as we learned with the idea of the "self-fulfilling prophecy theory." There is a greater purpose waiting on the other side of you in getting back up. Remember the passion of your youth before you let the trials of life paralyze you. If you do, your latter days will undoubtedly be greater than your former ones!

"Well Sarah, I don't know how to… even if I wanted to, I just can't find a way through. I don't see how?" Sis, just try! No more excuses? Just practice standing, then walking, then running. One day, you will be soaring! A vision is just a vision without goals in place on how to get there. Have a vision, but implement the strategy on how to obtain that vision. A vision without goals is to be a dreamer, only ever dreaming. The most successful people in the world have goals. They have daily, monthly, quarterly, and annual goals. They have benchmarks and tools to assess their success in reaching their milestones. Set goals to keep yourself on track. You will get to where you are going much faster if you intentionally hold yourself accountable. Miss a goal, set it again. Miss it again, set it again and again and again until you pass them! If you believe that failure is not an option, it won't be. Don't settle for failure. Set yourself up for success!

My tennis coach is Rusty Komori. He is famous in the sport of tennis and in my home state for leading Punahou School to an unprecedented 22 consecutive state championships. He still holds the national record in all sports for that achievement. He is also the author of, "Beyond the Game," a book that focuses on helping its readers achieve peak performance in business, sports, and life. He has been my tennis coach for over 15 years.

Rusty obviously coaches state champions, and I am not one of them. I have often joked with him that I am his goodwill project. And although he has improved my tennis game immensely, it is still, not the best. He has, for whatever reason, continued to coach me. He calls me his "Warrior." We have a compilation of tennis photos, all of me lying down in the middle of playing the game. I play until I am so exhausted that I have no more to give. I get back up and do it over and over again, until I am almost ready to pass out. I may not have the talent in tennis, but I have the determination and persistence to play until I can give no more to the sport. Perhaps he sees that I value him, his talent, and his time. I display this by being that *"Warrior."* I don't have to be the best. I just have to do my best and be willing to get back up time and time again. If you let it, persistence will make up where your talent cannot. Don't allow talent to stop you from achieving success. Success isn't won overnight. It is in the consistency of persevering.

Several years ago, I was working on a business deal. I didn't see how it was going to get closed. I couldn't see the way forward. Naturally, it looked challenging and unpromising. Somehow, I had a level of faith that things would work just as they needed to, so I had a persistent determination to meet my end goal. I didn't know how, but I trusted in the process and went for it in a major way. It was a negotiation. I negotiated from a position of faith and believed that I would get a favorable outcome.

During that time, one night, when I was sleeping, I dreamed that I was jumping off a cliff, and as I did, I would have the wings built to catch me on the way down. As I took the leap of faith, I would begin to soar with wings and I certainly did.

If it's impossible, remember to have faith and believe you can soar too! You don't always have to know how. Sometimes you just have to be willing. "How," will often become clear as you work through it. I strongly believe in jumping into things and believing that the wings needed to carry the vision will come, just as the faith required to take the first leap had. Coco Chanel once stated, "If you were born without wings, do nothing to prevent them from growing." So don't allow limiting mindsets to stop you from pursuing your dreams and soaring. A little bit of faith can carry you a long way. A little bit of persistence will get you to the finish line.

In August of 1780, during the Revolutionary War, the Southern American Army was destroyed by the British. There were about 1600 soldiers left within this army, all of which barely had clothes and arms. This was the main army left to defend the Southern Colonies. At this time, George Washington sent a man, by the name of General Nathaniel Greene south, with orders to remedy this all but hopeless situation. General Greene took over a defeated army, outnumbered two to one by the British, who were the best soldiers in the world at the time and were each equivalent to at least two American Militiamen. Greene was supposed to defend the south but was driven North by the British, where Greene continuously struck the British with hit-and-run attacks. These types of attacks were used by inferior armies unable to stand and defend their territory.

When retreating to the North, Greene's army had the ability to re-supply and restrengthen so they could go back and fight again. They then counter-attacked the British Army at Guilford Courthouse. By then, Greene's army had swollen to 4100 men and now outnumbered the British. As they retreated, they gained supplies and reinforcements. Green lost this battle at Guilford Courthouse, but inflicted twice as many casualties on the British than he suffered, forcing the British army to run for the coast. This pattern repeated itself many times over as Greene wrecked the British Army in the South.

Although Greene never officially won a battle, he reconquered the entire South except for Savanah and Charleston by decimating the British army. He would inflict almost twice as many casualties in each battle. At one point, he wrote to Washington lamenting, "We fight, get beat, rise and fight again!" No matter how many defeats he suffered, Greene got right back up and attacked again, and again and again. Although he did not win the battles, he ultimately won the campaign and helped America to win the Revolutionary War.

Can you imagine how defeated he must have been? To be a General in that era and to lose even one battle was humiliating and hope-deflating, but to lose every single battle and have the grit and persistence to go back and fight again and again for something that was so much greater than himself.

That kind of valor is our history, is your history, and your country. No matter where you come from or where you were born. In America, this is your heritage. This is your inheritance. By getting back up each time, Greene's army got stronger and better, and his reputation preceded him. The British never wanted to fight him and lost heavy casualties as a result.

Don't allow lost battles to overshadow the campaign. You may have been outnumbered, poorly equipped, and overlooked. You may have lost so many battles that you stopped counting, had your hope stripped from you, and you may have even been humiliated. But, you have been miscalculating your wins by counting the battles you have lost, failing to see the more significant picture before you. You may not see it, but you are growing. You are stronger, becoming reinforced, and you are winning the campaign! You getting back up and choosing to fight is changing the trajectory of your future and rewriting how the world will tally your losses. Your consistent perseverance will get you to the finish line. Your story is not done! It is being written in this very moment, and your outcome will not be the summation of the battles you lost, but of the war, you will ultimately win. "We fight, get beat, rise and fight again!" GIRL! FIGHT, GET BEAT, RISE, REPEAT, and FIGHT AGAIN! Now let me add, OVERCOME and WIN! Girl, it's time to GET BACK UP!

Chapter 13

THE GREATEST
GENERATION OF WOMEN

THE "GI GENERATION," ALSO KNOWN AS THE "WORLD WAR II
Generation," was defined as the generation of people born
from 1901-1927, and was also known as the "Greatest Generation"
to have ever lived. According to Wikipedia,

> *An early usage of the term The Greatest Generation was in
> 1953 by U.S. Army General James Van Fleet, who had recently
> retired after his service in World War II and leading the Eighth
> Army in the Korean War. He spoke to Congress, saying, "The
> men of the Eighth Army are a magnificent lot, and I have
> always said the greatest generation of Americans we have ever
> produced." The term was further popularized by the title of
> a 1998 book by American journalist Tom Brokaw. In the
> book, Brokaw profiled American members of this generation
> who came of age during the Great Depression and went on to
> fight in World War II, as well as those who contributed to the*

war effort on the home front. Brokaw wrote that these men and women fought not for fame or recognition, but because it was the «right thing to do».

For most of you, this will be the generation of your Grandparents or your Great Grandparents. This was a generation that was born during World War 1 and the Progressive Era. They lived through the "Golden Age of Hollywood," lived in the "Roaring '20s," saw the technological advancements of the telephone, the radio, and the automobile, lived through the Spanish Influenza and World War 2, the Dustbowl and the Banking Crisis of 1933, and saw the incredible rise of wealth within our country, only to be followed by the Great Stock Market Crash of 1929.

Through all of this, they persevered and became known as the "Greatest Generation" to have ever lived, and they were a beautiful and progressive generation. They loved deeply, and it was a romantic time when people loved, endured, and thrived through adversity. Out from it sprang the blues, jazz, swing dancing, and some of the most beautiful art that we know today, such as Pablo Picasso, Salvador Dali, and Georgia O'Keeffe.

My Grandfather came from this era, and I had the privilege of getting to know him a little before he passed. I've heard many stories about him, and everyone who knew him said he was a good man with a great heart. He fought in World War 2 for a cause that was greater than himself. He was called to serve, and he did so for his country. He fought for his brothers in arms and fought by them at the battle of D-Day, in Normandy, France, and also at the Battle of the Bulge, where he was wounded, at the turning point of World War 2. He was one of the few that got to come back home.

This generation knew what it was like not only to have to survive and adapt, but also to love. I remember being told that my Grandfather was madly in love with my Grandmother, and I even had the chance to witness it to a degree when I was younger. She was sick in the latter part of her life, and he would stroll her around in a wheelchair everywhere, and he would not go where she did not. Upon her death, my Grandfather couldn't live without her and followed shortly after. He did not want to be without her and therefore chose not to. It is said of him that he died of a broken heart. I wish I had more time with him, and I always said that was the kind of love I wanted to have: A love that was so deep that it could drown out the trials of this world, bring hope to future generations, and survive the transitions in adapting and overcoming. I want to bring that back into this world! I want to live and love deeply! I want to dream and persevere! They loved, and they lived, and they dreamed, and they persevered. They were the generation that *overcame*!

How many love stories do you know of that are told of this beautiful generation? The trial and hardships endured only made for greater perseverance and deeper love stories. The measure of who they were, was seen by the generations after them, and their legacy is carried out even today as we remember them as the "*Greatest Generation*" that had ever lived.

I believe that we, too, can become like them. I believe in my generation and the ones to follow, and I believe that we can, like them, overcome! What is life without faith? I have faith in us!

Faith is the substance of things hoped for, and it is the evidence of things not seen. The Z generation, Millennials, and Gen X have faced much adversity. Many of us lived through 911, the Afghanistan War from beginning to end, Isis in the Middle East, the creation of the Internet and the apathy along with it, the identity crisis facing our youth, the 2008 and 2009 Debt Crisis, sky-high inflation, Hurricane Katrina, trillions of dollars in debt inheritance that we didn't spend, wars beginning to erupt that we didn't start, shootings in schools, and houses with prices that have been crippling our youth, corrupt governments and yes of course, lockdowns, Covid 19 and extreme inflation.

We are not sure what kind of country we will be inheriting or leaving behind. We have seen everything that has tried to break our generations and steal our voices. We have also inherited disastrous public policies with absolutely irresponsible and out-of-control government spending. For the most part, everyone has been waiting… waiting for the next generation to stand up, stand strong, and take the reins.

The Boomer Generation is looking to retire. They have amassed a ten trillion-dollar portfolio in business ownership alone, with over 12 million companies and 25 million people hired under them. The greatest wealth transfer will occur with the exit of this generation, and they are forecasted to exit between now and the next decade or so. They are beginning to age out and orchestrate their succession plan. But as the Millennials and younger generations blame the Baby Boomer Generation for the debt crisis and absent parenting, so too does the Boomer Generation blame the younger generations for being entitled and unable to step into their roles to succeed them.

This was, in essence, the same parental dialogue followed by the Silent and Greatest Generation as well. The Greatest Generation fought to overcome. The Silent and Boomer Generations inherited their hard work. They reaped the rewards of affordable housing and geopolitical stability. The silent generation that came before the Boomers, wishes they wouldn't have been, as my Aunt, who came from that generation stated, "perhaps so *silent*." They watched as the thriving financial landscape of what was the "quintessential American life (this aside from certain deplorable social inequalities of course)" began to dissolve and progress downward. So, we are all still waiting for the next "Greatest Generation" to arise.

Birthed from the "Greatest Generation," the Boomers, although inheriting a nation at its prime, did work hard to create what they had built and sustain what they had inherited. They are the generation who built their company in the back of their garage. But without a bridge to the younger generations and vice versa, their legacies may die with them as a less-than-ideal asset sale, devalued ESOP (employee stock ownership plan) exit if they even qualify, or institutional ownership sale. Since over 80-90% of their wealth is estimated to be tied up in their businesses, this could present a problem. The younger generations could, as a result, miss out on the opportunity for multigenerational ownership.

Also to be noted is that if certain companies have not been able to advance technologically, the Boomers will not be able to remain competitive enough to even warrant a sale, as the country will see the largest wealth transfer of all time… and all at once, with this proposed ten trillion-dollar exit. Private banking will not be able to absorb these transactions and finance this amount of capital debt. We are already seeing insolvency and liquidity issues within our banking systems today, and I would infer that there will be some fire sales as a result.

In the history of the United States, it has never been a more favorable time to be a woman. We are no longer fighting for the women's suffrage movement, and Harvey Weinstein was put in jail! The women before us have paved the way, and we are reaping the benefits. We are not weak, nor are we incapable, and there is nothing that we cannot do if we put our minds to it. Work environments are more understanding of the balancing acts of being a mother, and women are being highlighted and brought up as business leaders in the entrepreneurial space like never before. It's also easier as a woman to get government-backed loans, contracts, and grants.

Being a woman has never been better, and there just aren't any excuses anymore. That does not mean there aren't trials and adversity, masculine toxicity, and misogyny we have to deal with. That just means we don't really have to play the victim as we once did. We can choose to overcome and be better than what we were served in the past. We can also choose how we treat our counterparts, the men in our society, and cheer the women around us. We are approaching an era where we will see the rise of female leadership across every sector. I believe when women are involved, we make things better and that will positively impact business. This means there will be some great moments for women in this arena in the coming decades, and if we position ourselves well, we will not only benefit in a great way but positively impact our future generations in the right way.

We will also have some unique opportunities to bridge the gap between the Boomer Generation and the Millenial Generation. Perhaps it would be insightful to learn from those who came before us. The Silent Generation, the generation between the "Boomers," and the "Greatest Generation," is on its way out, and we should ask them for mentorship before they go. We should ask them to share their stories and teach us what it was like to see the "Greatest Generation" that came before them. We should ask them their secrets, on what worked and what didn't.

We need healthy mentorship for our younger generations, and we need to build bridges with the older ones. We need to find wisdom to unlock the doors that are in front of us, with sometimes keys, that are only possessed by the ones who have opened them before us. We need to be able to humble ourselves, sit a while and learn how to glean.

We can be a *great generation*, but we will have to be willing to listen and become educated. We will have to be willing to observe and put into action what we learn. We will have to be willing to fight and persevere and get back up every time we fall. We have to be willing not to be a victim of our circumstances or surroundings but instead, find innovative ways to break through and become overcomers like the ones that came before us. We, too, can become the next "Greatest Generation!"

Chapter 14

BE THE BRIDGE

A BRAHAM LINCOLN, OUR PRESIDENT FROM 1861 TO 1865, once said, "America will never be destroyed from the outside. If we falter and lose our freedoms, it will be because we destroyed ourselves." President Lincoln meant those words, and he sacrificed his life to unite a country that was deeply divided, and that division was coming from within. It led to the greatest loss of life this country has ever seen in a single war. He took the words that Thomas Jefferson wrote in the Declaration of Independence, "We hold these truths to be self-evident, that all men are created equal," to heart. He fought to see the slavery that contradicted that reality be eradicated, as the plague it was to our nation.

My very many Greats' Grandfather fought as an Artillery General for the Union army at the Battle of Gettysburg, for which we have a street named after him on that Historic Battlefield called Hunt Avenue. Gettysburg became another turning point for another significant war, the Civil War, in which this Great Grandfather fought at. We lost an estimated 51,000 lives that day, in what was the bloodiest battle of the Civil War, in what was deemed the bloodiest war in the history of America. Over 2% of the population, or 620,000 lives, with some even saying as many as 880,000, were lost in that war. Today that would equate to over 6 million casualties, adjusted for the increase in population. Brothers were forced to fight against their brothers, and cousins their cousins, in a time when our country was divided and certainly destroying itself from within. President Abraham Lincoln could see firsthand how division from within could destroy our great nation.

On August 28[th,] 1963, on the footsteps of The Lincoln Memorial, dedicated in remembrance of President Abraham Lincoln himself, Martin Luther King Jr. gave the speech that changed the history of America as we know it. He gave the famous "I Have a Dream" speech.

Exert from "I Have a Dream" Speech August 28, 1963
Martin Luther King Junior

I have a dream today. I have a dream that one day every valley shall be exalted, every hill and mountain shall be made low, the rough places will be made plain, and the crooked places will be made straight, and the glory of the Lord shall be revealed, and all flesh shall see it together. This is our hope. This is the faith that I go back to the South with. With this faith we will be able to hew out of the mountain of despair a stone of hope. With this faith we will be able to transform the jangling discords of our nation into a beautiful symphony of brotherhood. With this faith we will be able to work together, to pray together, to struggle together, to go to jail together, to stand up for freedom together, knowing that we will be free one day. This will be the day when all of God's children will be able to sing with a new meaning, "My country, 'tis of thee, sweet land of liberty, of thee I sing. Land where my fathers died, land of the pilgrim's pride, from every mountainside, let freedom ring." And if America is to be a great nation this must become true. So let freedom ring from the prodigious hilltops of New Hampshire. Let freedom ring from the mighty mountains of New York. Let freedom ring from the heightening Alleghenies of Pennsylvania! Let freedom ring from the snowcapped Rockies of Colorado! Let freedom ring from the curvaceous slopes of California! But not only that; let freedom ring from Stone Mountain of Georgia! Let freedom ring from Lookout Mountain of Tennessee! Let freedom ring from every hill and molehill of Mississippi. From every mountainside, let freedom ring.

In 1968, Martin Luther King Jr was assassinated. This was a stain in our country's history with the sacrifice of another great man, on the altar of freedom, to bridge this nation. Walter Earl Brown wrote one of the most moving and passionate songs I have ever heard and it is called, "If I Can Dream." It was written for Elvis Presley after the death of Martin Luther King Jr, on the cusp of a once again very divided nation.

You have to hear it to bring the words to life and hear the ringing heartbreak in Elvis Presley's voice as he fights to sing it with every ounce of passion he has. I encourage you to play it with the reading of this chapter. The song was released in 1968, just two months after the assassination of Martin Luther King Jr, and was written for Elvis because Walter knew of the fondness that the King had for another "Great King." He wrote it in the likeness of Martin Luther King Jr's "I Have a Dream" speech, and when Elvis sang it, it was said that he had never sung with more passion than when he sang that song. It wrecks me every time I listen to it. I can feel his pain for his fellow brothers and sisters, our fellow brothers and sisters.

Elvis Presley was a bridge to a hurting nation at a time when our country was terribly divided over segregation. Almost 160 years after the Civil War ended and over 60 years after segregation ended, we still see the pain of a broken nation with people just needing to be heard and healed: A people, who feel as though they are unseen and a country that feels as though it just can't breathe. It is as though the sins of our past have been waiting to be resolved, and the healing can't be brought forth without the recognition of the voices that were not willing to be heard.

Once again, we find ourselves divided and unable to move forward. Only this time, the gap has widened. This time, it isn't just black or white, but Republican and Democrat, him vs her, LGBTQ vs. straight, pro-life vs. pro-choice, Boomers vs. Millennials, rich vs. poor...

If you are wondering, I am not a Republican or a Democrat. I am a, *human* who cares for other *humans*. What if we began to look at people like they were people again? What if we didn't have to always fight for our right to have the last word? What if we humbled ourselves toward each other and began to love our neighbor again? What if we began to see the other person as another human being, without any superiority or privilege over them? What if we chose to just *do better*?

Judging someone because they're different doesn't make them wrong. It makes you uncompassionate and mean. It makes you a bully. It shows the deficiency in you and not them. People don't grow up wanting not to fit in and not know who they are or why they believe the things they do. Neither do they grow up wanting to be confrontational or different. The world can be a cruel place and do cruel things to people. We don't even know the back story of those we judge, what they struggled through, and what the world did to them.

When we judge, we fail to see the heart of another human being. We only see the label. Instead of wanting to help someone heal, we want to be the ones to cast the first stone towards anyone that doesn't look like us, talk like us, or think like us, but that won't bring healing to a divided nation. It will only further divide an already broken country.

We all make mistakes, and no one is without them, but what if we pivoted as a nation to just "see each other" again? That means we are willing to recognize the pain and see a hurting nation. That means we are willing to see our wrongs, humble ourselves and make things right. If we can see it, we can heal it. If we can dream it, we can achieve it! I haven't always been proud to own my past viewpoints. And that's ok. I choose to do better now. Choose with me to do better! It's never too late to heal and make past wrongs right!

We are divided again, and I do believe that the only way that America the Great will fall is from within. But from within, we can also become united and find strength! We look divided to the world, and the world has not always loved America. There are those that would desire to see our country fallen. We look weak during a time when it is far too dangerous to look weak. I have traveled a bit, and the world is not fond of who we are at this moment in time, and if we are not careful, those watching will find opportunities to act against our shining beacon of light.

In 2022, I had the privilege of going to Israel as a delegate for the United States on a humanitarian assignment. I have seen firsthand what a politically driven, divided country looks like. I had the opportunity to go with some diplomats into the West Bank, which is largely under Palestinian territory. Towns are segregated by Jewish or Palestinian control. We were escorted in and we visited a farm in Samaria where a family from the United States was living. They were living in one of the Jewish towns. Right next to them was a Palestinian town, and at night it got ugly, bombs would be fired, and trees would be set on fire.

Jewish towns were abutting these Palestinian towns, and if you were Jewish, by law, you would not be able to enter a Palestinian town and vice versa, unless you were on an assignment like we were. License plates would also differentiate you by your ethnicity.

These people are all Israeli and are all from the same nation, and yet division has been woven into their very fabric of life. Going there and seeing the country divided into segments by ethnicity was painstaking, and the parallels of where we could go as a nation became very real on that trip. I saw hate up close and personal, and it broke my heart. My heart wept for Israel, as a home to both the Jewish and Muslim people. As I drove through their divided country, I began to think, what would it take to heal this hurting nation and be the bridge to peace?

I was reminded of the time when I had driven through the cities of Louisville and St. Louis after the fatal shootings that rocked our nation. Our country was divided and in pain, and so too was theirs. So, what would it take to build a bridge from the West Bank and Palestine to Jerusalem? I don't know. But I believe that if we can dream it, we can begin to achieve it. I believe it starts with seeing people as people. If we begin to value people again and put away our agendas, we will stop seeing each other as an agenda and see people as humans again with feelings. I believe when we start to see and understand emotions, we can answer with compassion. From there, we can go forward as a nation to heal the sins of our past.

We aren't what political parties try to define us as. We are so much more than their labels and agendas. We are a nation that can do great things, and if you allow yourself to strip off the price tag that someone else paid for you, let them know that you are not for sale anymore. Because you can't afford to be divided, and they can't afford to pay for you anymore. Your value has just increased, and you are priceless! You have great things to do, and this world needs you to dream again! Just being healed isn't enough anymore. There are others just like you that are needing to be brought up and *you* will be the one to bring them up!

Remember when I started with, *"When you get up, bring one up."* Mother Theresa said, "If you can't feed the whole world, just feed one." So, get up! This world needs you to just start with one. Staying down is the most selfish thing you can do for yourself, your family, and the future people that you will impact. That is what Chapter 6, "Purpose Driven," is all about. I am trying to get you to think outside of who you are. I am trying to get you to get out of your self-inflicted prison and dream of more than your own contentment, your own healing, and your own life. There is something on the other side of you getting up. So, dream big! What nation is on the other side of your purpose? Who will you build that bridge to, to bring healing to the world?

Because of what you went through, who can you see that no one else can see? Who can you build a bridge to that no one else will? Now, influence the world with that vision. Bring hope and make it contagious! Hope deferred makes the heart weak, so allow for your hope to thrive again! As Elvis referenced, be that candle out there in a dark world, and let your dream begin to be ignited! Be the flame that starts the fire!

Chapter 15

_____

VERSION 2.0

WE BEGAN THIS BOOK BY GOING ON A JOURNEY TOGETHER. I shared you mine, in the hope that you might be encouraged in yours. I can share with you. I can be with you, and I can encourage you, and become your biggest cheerleader. I can also get up with you. What I can't do is *get up for you*. You are going to have to hate the excuses to rise above them. Remember that you are stronger than what you have been told. You are stronger than what happened to you, and you are stronger than who you think you are.

The mistakes, the excuses, the labels, the failures…. Begin to replace them with the grace, the determination, the freedom, and the victory that will carry you forward into being the overcomer that you were called to be. Stop waiting for someone to come around to save you. Free yourself from every form of victim mentality. Encourage, forgive, and surround yourself with who you want to become, and don't look to this world for your happiness and joy. That all comes from within.

Begin to map out who your "Who" is. Begin to map out what

your purpose and destiny are, what you're working towards, and what you're fighting for. What drives your passion? Your destiny and calling can't afford for you to stay stagnant nor be consumed by your regrets and memories. Being a female entrepreneur is tough, and you're going to need to be that lion, in order to make it out of that jungle alive!

We all know the beloved Warner Bros movie, "The Wizard of Oz," with Judy Garland as Dorothy. In The Wizard of Oz, the Cowardly Lion goes on a journey to find his courage. He believes that he isn't able to be a true lion and help others in times of need without finding his courage. In the movie, he meets Dorothy, Scarecrow, and Tinman, who tells him that maybe the Wizard in the Emerald City could help him find the courage he needed to be a lion. So, he goes along the yellow brick road, thinking that the Wizard will be able to help him find his courage. When meeting him for the first time, the Wizard of Oz tells them to kill the Wicked Witch of the West, and upon doing so, he will then grant them their wishes. They do as the Wizard tells them to, and through the journey, they display courage in the many perils they face along the way, including killing the Wicked Witch.

When they finally came back to the Wizard with the news that they had completed their task, they found that the Wizard was just a man hiding behind the curtain, pretending to be the Great Wizard of Oz, and they asked him, "What about the courage that you promised the Cowardly Lion." The wizard then said,

"As for you my fine friend, you are a victim of disorganized thinking. You are under the unfortunate thinking that simply

because you run away from danger, you have no courage. You are confusing courage with wisdom. Back where I come from, they have men there we call heroes. Once a year they take their fortitude out of mothballs and parade it down the main street of the city, and they have no more courage than you have. But, they have one thing that you haven't got, a medal. Therefore, for meritorious conduct, extraordinary valor, conspicuous bravery against wicked witches, I award you the triple cross. You are now a member of the Legion of Courage."

The Wizard couldn't magically transform the Lion or put him under a spell to make him more courageous. He was just a man. He simply told him what he needed to hear, "that his thinking was wrong."

This story illustrates that just because someone has run from danger does not mean it is the same as being a coward. He said that to run from danger is to have wisdom and does not equate to cowardice. When it really mattered, the Cowardly Lion fought and stood up for his friends. When confronted with the Wicked Witch, the Cowardly Lion was not so cowardly after all. When confronted with the danger surrounding his friends, he faced fear head-on and did not run from it. He was brave and just needed to be told that he was.

What you are looking for will not be found in any one person, title, or job. It is within you! If you look to this world, you may also find another *man or woman behind the curtain,* and it will disappoint you. You have to believe in who you are, and fight the self-limiting mindsets that combat the inner you. You have to know that you are more than capable of being the victor you have set out to become. I don't know who you are on the other side of reading this book, but I do believe I know what you are not, and you are not a coward! If you were, you would not be reading this book. You would not be willing to go back and re-examine the areas that had brought you down in the first place. Reading this book makes you face your fears and run into the storm! Being tired and weary and worn out doesn't make you a coward… it simply makes you *tired, weary,* and *worn out.*

You may have been caught up and overwhelmed by the storms a time or two and faced some fears that tried to drown you, but they didn't, and you are still here. You are more than they say you are, more than you think you are, and more than you say you are. It is not cowardly to have faced difficult obstacles that have set you back and have had the wisdom to discern the dangers.

We all go through the storms, and it takes courage to stand on the other side after coming through, even if you are reluctant through the process. It takes courage to get back up. It's not easy to get up time and time again as you have. It takes courage to be the strong woman that you are, overcoming what you have overcome. It takes courage just to stand sometimes, and *you,* my Sister, have that courage. You not only have the courage to stand, but you have the courage to walk, to run, to dream, and to leap! Let this book be your medal of courage and honor. Let it be the reminder that you are overcoming, that you will overcome and become the *overcomer*!

You have been fighting for a long time Sis, and it is time that you are recognized not for your failures but it is time that you are recognized for your victories. It is time that YOU recognize that you are the victor. And "*as for you, my fine friend,*" you may have been a victim of disorganized thinking just like the Cowardly Lion, but cowardly he is no more, and neither are you. It is time to let that chapter, that season, and that era go!

I began writing this book by telling you that it took everything just to come back to you, and it did. It really did. It set back into motion the storms I had run from my whole life because ignoring them never made them disappear. It took introspection that was hard to want to do, and it took realities that were hard for me to face. I had to face the storm, run into it and come out with the sun shining on the other side. The storm of feeling defeated will no longer overwhelm me, and I now know what I am fighting for. I am fighting for you, on the other side of this book, and everything that I am called to.

I am fighting for my legacy, my children, and my purpose. I know the importance of me getting back up, and I am finishing this book stronger, more determined, and able to leap into my calling, my destiny, and my purpose. I made a choice, and I allowed the process to take place. I didn't have to know how. I just had to be willing, willing to get back up one more time. And if takes another time, I will get up again, again and again! I will get up as long as it takes for me to get to the finish line of life! I will not stop fighting to get back up. I did it, am doing it, and I'm doing it with you, and so can you!

In chapter one, I shared the anthem for women, "I am Woman, Hear me Roar," sung by Helen Reddy. Over 40 years later, Katy Perry wrote a tribute to the 1972 anthem called "Roar." She wrote the song during a challenging time in her life. It was written in response to a transition in her career alongside a divorce she was going through, where she felt like she had lost her voice. According to Sabrina Chitty's article, "Roar," by Katy Perry," Katy Perry states, *We ourselves are our biggest bully* as we stand in our own way. "Roar" ultimately is about not letting anyone, even yourself, stand in your way of success and relationships." If that's you, it's time to get out of your way and remove the obstacles blocking you from your success!

You may have been like Katy Perry sang about in the song. You may have been held down. You may have been pushed past the breaking point. You may have gone through the storm. You may have even felt like you were a zero at times! You may have been pressed, and you may have had to go through that refining fire! However, you are getting your voice back!

Girl, it's time to brush off that dust because you are not crushed. And girl...you dance through that refining fire because you comin' out like a diamond. You have learned what it is to become that fighter, and your voice? Yes, Sis! It will shake the ground like thunder. You've found the eye of the LION, and you are the champion! Girl, you are gettin' your "ROAR" back, and your roar WILL be louder than any other Lion! YOU are coming back, yes YOU! But you are coming back differently. You are coming back as the bigger, badder version of who you used to be. Say hello to the new 2.0 you! Say hello to your new "ROAR!" Girl, You are getting back up again and finding your voice! Congratulations Sis! You are the overcomer!

Twenty five percent of royalties received will go to the 501c3 Foundation, Let Love Be Greater. One hundred percent of those proceeds will be strictly designated to the aid and scholarships for women and children in need

L et Love be Greater is a 501c3 organization that believes love is the answer. That love takes action and builds bridges to difficult places. A bridge has the ability to unify, connect and close the divide. "Let Love Be Greater" wants to be the bridge to give women a hope, a future, and an opportunity to let their hearts take flight and dream again!

The organization offers economic and entrepreneurial scholarship opportunities to women needing financial assistance, specifically displaced and exploited women and children. The organization's objectives are to support those disproportionately affected by their trials and circumstances and to aid them in rebuilding their identity as future independent community and business leaders. "Let Love Be Greater" provides a community that supports personal development and growth so that women and children can reignite their purpose and get them to dream again.

Let Love be Greater has worked with various organizations on elevating women and children and combating sex trafficking and is always looking for new opportunities to develop new partnerships.

To learn more about the organization, support and/or directly provide a scholarship to women and children in need, please visit the website

www.letlovebegreater.com

If you are also interested in getting in touch with the author for future motivational speaking engagements and press-related inquiries, the website provided will also offer the appropriate channels to do so.

Made in the USA
Las Vegas, NV
24 October 2023